Foreword by "Jesus of Nazaretn," Autnor oi the Bible

MASTERING MUSTARD SEED MOTIVATION

"Seven Key Imperatives"
The Why, How, and Purpose of MSM,
Plus, a Surprise or Two

[signature]

PROV. 11:30-31

ROBERT HUGH PARK

Mastering Mustard Seed Motivation
"Seven Key Imperatives" The Why, How, and Purpose of
MSM, Plus, a Surprise or Two
by Robert Hugh Park

Printed in the United States of America

ISBN 9781619042704

Italics in all Scripture quotations reflect the author's added emphasis.

Every story in this book is an account of an actual event. No composite anecdotes or fiction techniques have been used. However, details in some stories have been modified to improve readability or to protect privacy.

Mastering Mustard Seed Motivation: Seven Key Imperatives, the Why, How and Purpose of MSM, Plus a Surprise or Two / Robert Hugh Park — 1st ed.

Includes bibliographical references.

Also available in:
Hardcover
eBook:

www.xulonpress.com

Dedication

To The Lost and Needy of this World
and
our Children, their mates, and fabulous Grandchildren
Toni, (Bruce) Kelly (Ronald) Sandra (Robert)
Aaron, Andrew, and Amy
Lauren and Michael
Scott, Christopher, Jonathan, and Sean

CONTENTS

FOREWORD, by *"Jesus of Nazareth," Author of
the Bible* xi

INTRODUCTION
MMSM Purpose Statement, *Sensing the "Why, How
and Purpose" of MSM* xv

*Part 1: Believing Faith, Obedient Love, Your
Heart's Desire, Showing Loving Faith —*
"Transformation Time" 23
    1. A New Belief – *Without this, the story ends
      horribly*.. 26
    2. A Spirit of Obedience – *You disappear and
      HE takes charge*.. 41
    3. A Seeking Heart – *A Thirst for Truth*.............. 54
    4. A Desire to Demonstrate Faith – *Love
      takes over in spades*...................................... 61

*Part 2: Speaking out Courageously, Acting
on God Inspired Direction, Pray without Ceasing —*
"Action Time" 69
    5. A Courageous Willingness to Speak out –
      Fear is a thing of the past.............................. 73
    6. A Move to Godly Action on His Promptings –
      The first 5 Imperatives in Action 83

7. A Continual Spirit of Prayer – *The central
   Key that UNLOCKS Faith* 89

*Part 3: The Applied Dynamics of the Christian Life —
"Biblical Men and Women, under the Control
and Care of the Master"* 101

8. Challenges We All Face –*"Whether a New or
   Mature Christian" A veritable potpourri of
   human experience... in no special order* 103
   The Beginning 106
   Peering Deeply 109
   Worldly Worries 110
   Falsehood 113
   Will it be Pride... or, Gratefulness? 117
   Assumptions 120
   Total Dependence 122
   Sounding the Trumpet 128
   Where does the Church fit in? 130
   Holiness 150
   Are Answers really Answers? 152
   Do not Despair...I am There 154
   Categorizing People 155
   What are You? 157
   Claiming the shoes of Others 158
   Physical Corruption 159
   God's Holy Tissue 161
   Nine and Ten 162
   All will Know! 164
   Who is Wise? 166
   Crumble or Live? 169
   Terminal, what Is... and what Isn't? 170
   Just words, Hmmm? – No Way! 171
   Senior Power 172
   God's Anti-biotic... the Bible 176
   Redemption 180
   A Pair of Glasses 182

Spirituality, the Unseen Truth 183
Summation 185

Part 4: *'Living' Accounts of Choice Servants of God —*
"Both Historical and Contemporary," All in subjection
to the Word of God, followed by... The End of Life
as we know It – "It's God's Judgment Time" 187

9. MSM filled lives...Up to the Brim! — *"Real*
   Stories and Real People, Who walked the
   Walk, and talked the Talk, and made
   Music from the Word of God." 189
   Job 191
   Matthew 193
   John the Baptist 195
   The Apostle John 199
   The Apostle Peter 202
   The Apostle Paul 206
   James, *the brother of Jesus* 208
   Harold Ray Henniger 210
   George Beauchamp Vick 213
   Fanny Crosby 216
   Jerry Falwell 217
   Wally Stuchul 220
   Verne Hugh Park 222

10. When Time is no More! – *"Life as we know*
    it ceases to be" 226
    "The Judgment Seat of Christ" 226
    "The Day of the Lord" 230
    "Our Faithful God" 233

Epilogue: *We Begin to Finish — "This is where*
YOU hit the road!" 237

Notes 241

Acknowledgements 243

FOREWORD

By

"Jesus of Nazareth,"
Author of the Bible

The following words of Jesus Christ; taken from Matthew 13, are placed in this "Foreword," in such a manner, as to *"extend the call"* of Jesus in preparing the minds and hearts of ALL people, *not just those he was directly speaking to,* through His use of parables, but also a challenge for them, to both intellectually and spiritually, begin to understand more about the Kingdom of Heaven, and His purpose for coming to Earth.

Jesus tells this first story, or parable, and then provides its meaning for each one so that none should have an excuse. Listen... just as if you were there standing in front of Him, and with an open mind seeking to distinguish what your own personal condition in life is. As you listen to Him speak, you'll soon discover His message is about "people who are seeking answers, or who are not." You'll also notice that He doesn't mince His words when it comes to the results of these two frames of mind.

The mere fact you have this book in your hand, should be an indication to Him of your desire to understand truth, and how it may apply to your own personal heart and mind.

As Jesus completes this Foreword, He is seeking your motivation to complete the reading of this book, as a way to take whatever next step is appropriate for you. *Listen to God speak through His Son, "Jesus Christ of Nazareth."*

That same day Jesus went out of the house and sat by the lake. Such large crowds gathered around him that he got into a boat and sat in it, while all the people stood on the shore. Then he told them many things in parables, saying: "A farmer went out to sow his seed. As he was scattering the seed, some fell along the path, and the birds came and ate it up. Some fell on rocky places, where it did not have much soil. It sprang up quickly, because the soil was shallow. But when the sun came up, the plants were scorched, and they withered because they had no root. Other seed fell among thorns, which grew up and choked the plants. <u>Still other seed fell on good soil, where it produced a crop—a hundred, sixty or thirty times what was sown</u>. Whoever has ears, let them hear."

The disciples came to Him and asked, "Why do you speak to the people in parables?"

He replied, "Because the knowledge of the secrets of the kingdom of heaven has been given to you, but not to them. Whoever has will be given more, and they will have an abundance. Whoever does not have, even what they have will be taken from them. This is why I speak to them in parables:

"Though seeing, they do not see; though hearing, they do not hear or understand.

In them is fulfilled the prophecy of Isaiah: 'you will be ever hearing but never understanding; you will be ever seeing but never perceiving. <u>For this people's heart has become calloused; they hardly hear with their ears, and they have closed their eyes. Otherwise they might see with their eyes, hear with their ears, understand with their hearts and turn, and I would heal them.</u>'

But blessed are your eyes because they see, and your ears because they hear. For truly I tell you, many prophets and righteous people longed to see what you see but did not see it, and to hear what you hear but did not hear it.

(Matthew 13:1-17) (Added emphasis)

If you seek God with an honest heart, He will remove any calluses' which might be there! If you're on the fence at this very moment, and do not understand, continue reading with an open mind and heart.

I guarantee you, by the promises found in the Word of God; you will spend eternity looking back with the realization that your heart was touched by the Spirit of God that day.

May God continue to bless you and yours, as you seek to know Him.

INTRODUCTION

MMSM – Purpose Statement

Sensing the "Why, How and Purpose" of MSM

W elcome to MMSM, a book whose purpose is to extend and amplify the message as portrayed in my book on faith... "MSM, Mustard Seed Motivation," a love story about my family, and how, through the power of God, their lives were changed in so many ways. What you'll read and understand in this sequel has been written for your encouragement as you seek greater understanding of the life and purpose of Jesus Christ, and His positive plan for your life.

If by chance, you haven't read MSM yet, allow me to share these following thoughts for you to do so, before discovering what MMSM is all about.

"Herein lives a love story painted and penned by the master of it all. His fingerprints may be lifted and proved to be the guiding hand of a family within the Family of God. His touch has been felt in unfathomable ways through time immemorial, including this short story of the Park family, a story, detailing God's love for you, and how He has a plan already in process, deep within your heart and mind. As you begin to sense the not so hidden soft touch of the Master at work, you also will begin to introspectively connect your life experience as He weaves His unmistakable love pattern into your heart. Allow this truth to bathe your spirit, and give rise to a new and lasting joy you so desperately seek, or, if you've come this way before, may the "God provided" reality of His presence, be an encouragement to brush away complacency, fear, heaviness of heart or anything which has stifled your God-given faith. Take heart... it's His heart He wants you to learn more about. The mere fact you have this book in your hands... reading these words, is proof of your earnest desire to know and experience His personal love for you."

Imagine... God loves ME! He wants to express
this personal gift to ME!
A gift; wrapped in His Word, the Bible,
and made real by the Holy Spirit!

We are privileged, beyond measure, to see and listen to His voice when His Word comes alive and begins to turn into believing faith in our future. As you absorb the truth of these "Magnificent Seven Imperatives," you will automatically begin the change of a lifetime.

There is another definition of MMSM... and it is equally applicable to this concept...

Mastering Magnetic Sacred Motives

Unfortunately, many of us, even if we are already believers, are not naturally drawn to the study of the Word of God, the Bible. God's main purpose for Christians is to share with everyone, the life and teaching of His Son Jesus Christ. Now, when God speaks and gives us this command, you'd think everyone couldn't wait to devour a Masterpiece written by the maker of the Universe. But no, we want to do our own thing until the

Spirit of God drags us to Himself, and in some cases... kicking and screaming at the very thought of it all!

We are also not 'naturally' drawn to seeking and reading the message God provides in His Bible, precisely because every one of us, from birth, is at odds with God! As sad as this may sound, it is an absolute fact which gained its legs by something as simple as rebellion, a rebellion which began in the Garden of Eden. *You know the story...*

Here's a legitimate analogy to consider. Don't you just hate it when your children rebel against you as a parent? Normally, our excuse for them may be... *"But, they are immature, don't know hardly anything yet, and haven't lived long enough to see the big picture as we do,"*... but then, why are all of us so rebellious in life, regardless of age? To be frank, after learning why this is true, while still a child, this weakness is only exceeded by our individual pride... a prideful attitude embedded in each of us as the result of "original sin." An unwanted gift applied to all future generations by the first individual to walk the face of earth... Adam.

This is 'deceitful pride' which drives our belief system, the actions we take, and the selfishness all of us are plagued with from birth.

I've said all of the above, hopefully to fertilize your interest in overcoming and not being controlled by this pride, and to gain a willingness to learn more about the God of the Bible, and His Son Jesus Christ.

There are still forces in this world whose purposes are to entice you away from truth. Every avenue of life on which we proceed, is infected with lies and false promises which are sweet to our taste and delightful to our sight and hearing! It's so easy to be hooked by these influences which promote the concept... life is all about ME; what I want and what I think I need, as opposed to what is truthful, what is right, and what is best for me as I learn of God's purpose for my life. Anything apart from this is worthless, because this life we have, is but a steppingstone into eternity. It only makes sense then, to focus on eternity instead of the "here and now."

When you see beyond your pride, your life here on this planet now takes on new meaning, joy and purpose.

The wonderful result... A potentially degrading life-style is changed into pure joy and happiness! A life filled with mental anguish is replaced with peace of mind. The pain of being alone is overwhelming until you learn the secret of having a personal friend, called the Holy Spirit walking with you. This is the truth of our relationship with Jesus Christ, but unless you open your heart and mind to this truth, you'll never know.

Friend, my effort with this book, as a sequel to MSM, is to provide you with a fulfilling, in-depth revelation of the (7) "Key Imperatives" of MSM. You'll have my best effort in providing supporting biblical scriptures and stories which paint a vivid picture of the power and value of each one of them. Imperatives, which in turn, as you put each one into practice in your life, will create a powerful [Magnetism] for these "New Sacred Motives;" motives, which God through His Word, wants us to enjoy personally, and to share with others as we walk through life in obedience and love for Him.

When you think of personal magnetism or magnetic personalities, the list is long and includes people from all walks of life. But without hesitation, Jesus Christ is at the head of the list. After living 33 short years, He accomplished what God the Father sent Him here to do. He has captured the hearts and minds of His children across the face of this globe unlike any other person in history! Think of it, even our calendar begins with His birth. Also, the work of those original Christian disciples and apostles is not over, and will not conclude until Jesus Christ, the Son of God, returns as Lord and Master of the Kingdom of God. The vivid truth is; thousands upon thousands are in the process of turning over their hearts and minds to the Savior on a daily basis! This is a clarion call to you as well.

As you read and study MMSM, God is looking for you to join the team!

"Mastering Mustard Seed Motivation," involves every part of your life, and your teacher, Jesus Christ, is the one who provided you with this life you have in the first place. What could be more important and what could be better, than to learn more, and have your life directed by Him!

Nothing... I say nothing has more impact, than the Word of God on each of our lives, whether we are believers or not. The Bible is unique in its ability to speak for itself. No amount of explanation, or attempt to clarify a given scriptural passage can compare to the opportunity we have in listening to God teach us by allowing scripture to answer our questions. Therefore, you will be experiencing this truth in your reading of this work. Don't allow Satan to dissuade you in reading the scriptures as they are presented. Here are some reasons to consider...

You will learn... reading the Bible is not a chore! It's an opportunity to listen to God Himself speak! *With that said, there is a difference between reading and studying the word of God.* When you simply 'read' the Word of God, you'll certainly be able to understand what you read... But, this is where God's Word is different from any other book available to you. Quickly, you'll grasp this truth; "Scripture interprets Scripture!" Whatever you read, for the most part in the Bible, is connected to other supporting documentation located in various parts of the book. This being true, you'll soon understand why the Bible may be "studied" like no other book you'll ever read. Therefore, don't fall into the trap of just reading portions of the Bible in so many days, weeks or months, just to be "reading" it. If you're not careful, the trap you fall into is thinking that God is pleased with you if you read His Word, only as a thing of duty. As His child, we certainly have a "duty" to be faithful in our learning process. But the process isn't expanded just by duty. Study, on the other hand, doesn't necessarily mean more work or more time, but it does result in a much higher level of understanding and appreciation for everything you read in this, His book. When we think of Bible scholars, we may think of specific kinds of people which have been called to study the Holy Scriptures almost every waking moment of their lives, maybe as a fulltime job. But realize this truth; there is not a person alive, that loves this book, and gives a reasonable amount of time in studying it, which cannot attain the title of being a Bible scholar. In reality, God is the only one who knows those who are genuine Bible scholars. It's not a title to attain, but an ability to be useful to God in the lives of others, as they seek to know Him.

Are you interested in expanding your knowledge? It's natural to buy books as a way of satisfying a hidden thirst for learning and experiencing something new. What we seem to not be aware of is this... it's a God-given drive, provided by Him immediately after we leave the womb. We want more than anything, just to "know!" To begin the process of a daily expansion of gray matter into what God has planned for us. Most are not aware of this "God driven" appetite for knowledge. Apart from His "Book of Knowledge," we believe that this growth is simply a "natural" human attribute, in no way connected to a loving Creator. All of life is just happenstance we think! We take shortcuts to knowledge by just letting "things" happen. We believe there's no personal design... "I'll just let 'osmosis' have its way." So, we go through life driven only by "inclination," not in concert with the creator and His plan and goal for our lives. Here's the real truth: There's a term which speaks to everyone who has ever lived. Never have there been two words spoken which characterizes our living reality more...!

Total Dependence

From the moment the first human being, Adam, was born, until the most recent birth has taken place, all have been totally dependent upon God for everything that is, or ever will be! Regardless of our relationships with family friends and most importantly, with God, our dependence upon him is undeniable. This subject is the essence of all life, and deserves to be discussed in detail with supporting evidence. For now, this being the Purpose Statement of MMSM, I look forward to sharing my heart with you about this dependency question. A question that can have only one answer, and on that answer, the whole universe hangs!

God's Perpetual Love in Action!

One last thought... there is a connection between Bible Study and Prayer. As you Study, as opposed to just reading, you'll soon discover a need to pray! This automatically is part of the "prompting" process God uses in His ongoing communication with you. I can't tell you how many times I've been caught up in a particular study, when the Spirit of God puts the brakes on, and I'm directed to pray about the connection of my study, and a need which only God can supply! Now, I call that..., "Gods perpetual Love in Action!" He's always right there with us... leading, guiding, explaining, teaching, directing, and through it all, demonstrating His uncommon Love in His uncommon way! Once you've understood this...What could be better? My job then, is to help you on your journey, by searching the

Word together in order to bring light to its message as it relates to the subject at hand. I have no greater joy than to be a conduit in your thinking process. May God become yours; you are already His, but my friend, joining the team is your free choice! Don't find yourself out in the cold, all alone... without hope for your eternal future.

> John 7:37 *(NKJV)*.... "If anyone thirsts, let him come to Me and drink."

One last comment, if you haven't read MSM yet, may I strongly suggest you STOP right now where you're at... get the book, read it, and then return. What you read here in MMSM will then take on a whole new perspective!

Also, be aware... you may find a few errors missed in the proof reading process of MSM. Since this was a "self published book," yours truly is to blame! Here's my take on this reality... I've made many errors in life, and have done my best to rid myself of them, but until I find myself in Heaven with my Savior, they'll be more along the way. Hopefully MMSM will be better!

MMSM - Mastering Mustard Seed Motivation

Part 1

Believing Faith
Obedient Love
Your Heart's Desire
Showing Loving Faith

"Transformation Time"

Note: All scripture references are italicized, and unless otherwise indicated, are taken from the NIV, 1984 Version

The following first four "Key Imperatives" are the cornerstone's of your personal, spiritual and educational relationship in preparation for an ongoing life, filled with your Lord and Savior, Jesus Christ.

What follows in Part #2, are the remaining three "Key Imperatives," which will define God's expectation for your life. You will learn how to recognize an untold number of miracles and what role God has planned for you, as His messenger to a lost and dying generation of His children.

Then, in Part #3, we will wade into the problems and difficulties of many life situations Satan uses to insure we are not what God wants us to be. This effort is not all inclusive. That would be a total impossibility! But, I do want to bring to mind a variety of actions and inactions which keeps us from running on all eight cylinders; things which may seem to be obvious, but which plague all of us, from time to time but with a little different twist!

Following in Part #4, will be a number of life stories, which should glue you to your chair as you soak up the self evident reality of MSM in all of its glory! These will include real life situations, and hopefully will connect to various biblical stories, in order to connect today with the people of the Bible.

The Epilogue will draw this puppy to a close! Your heart of hearts is what's at stake! The truth of the Word of God must be sought and digested, if life is to extend beyond the here and now. Of that... I'm sure!

Now... buckle your seat belt... God is speaking! I'm just the messenger.

CHAPTER 1

MSM - Key Imperative #1

A New Belief
Without this, the story ends horribly

["*You now have...a deep in the heart commitment to, and acceptance of, Jesus Christ the Son of God by simple faith in Him. You now have a belief in his life, death, and resurrection, and which is now at his Father's right hand, intervening in behalf of His children who are fully committed to Him.*"]

This all important initial step, *guaranteeing your eternity with Jesus Christ*, is then expanded and supported by the remaining Six Imperatives, allowing you to grow in the grace and knowledge of God and His son Jesus Christ. There will be the ability to learn how to forgive and to show love where love needs to be shown. You will begin to receive "<u>promptings and nudges</u>" from God as he directs you in a new godly way of life. And most of all, you will be amazed... over and over how God affects each day. You will wake up with new expectations for what will happen, and a "fear free" acceptance of what each day holds.

You are not alone anymore!

S uddenly, you find yourself wide-awake as you lay in bed as did I, some 51 years ago, but the reality seems like a frightening dream because you've never been down this path before! Your lovely wife is calling out to you pleading for help. Your mind is a blur as you attempt to make sense of this dream, or is it reality? Then the words you hear from her begin to make sense.

"Bob, my water has broken, and we need to get to the hospital as soon as possible!" she said, in hurried tones.

This was my experience many years ago, when Gale gave birth to our first baby girl, Toni Lynn. We arrived at the hospital without incident, and I knew it wouldn't be long until this message from God, in the form of a brand-new person, who would enter our lives, and change us for all eternity.

It was not an easy birth for Gale since it was her first child, but in just a few hours, which seemed like an eternity, I was ushered into her room where she cradled Toni in her arms, with the most wonderful look on her face, a look I will never forget.

Together we looked at this little gift from God in disbelief. We looked at those tiny little hands and feet, fingernails, eyelashes, and then later, when her eyes opened for the first time, it was as if we could see right into her heart, and mind. This was joy unspeakable! *This was the love of God in all of its glory!* This was OUR child! She was now an equal part of our family.

Toni gave new meaning and understanding for the word called love. *(More on this word in Part 3)* God provided the two of us the opportunity to create a never dying soul. She was an addition in the creation of His Universe. Here was a new life capable of unbelievable power and promise in the fulfillment of His plan for the world. *And, now, as I pen these words, this truth has, and is being fulfilled daily. (In chapter 22 of Mustard Seed Motivation, you've already learned much of what has happened in the life of Toni Lynn, along with Kelly and Sandy as well.)*

It was God the Father, God the Son Jesus, and God the Holy Spirit, along with multitudes of Angels in heaven, who experienced even greater joy when the "Second Birth" occurred in each of their lives, obviously much more than what Gale and I experienced in the physical birth of these three wonderful daughters.

We have had the joy in seeing all of them grow and mature physically and most importantly, spiritually. But we knew, before they were born, their second birth was more important than even the first. God taught us through His Word, to understand this in the lives of all of His children... the truth about life on earth, as a "Born Again Christian," is the knowledge we will someday be standing in front of the door to eternity, possessing the key to enter.

The second birth, "A new Belief"... is the [Key] to this door. This is the first and primary Imperative in living a life driven by the power of MSM.

The Second Birth

The second birth... is God the Father's plan for restoration and eternal life for all of His children. The Apostle Peter made this truth very clear, but before continuing, please let me to share this idea.

"When you read all of the "Biblical passages" presented to you in this book, *I suggest reading them out loud. If I could command you to do it this way, I would!* Believe me, in doing this, the meaning will be indelibly etched into your memory and understanding like nothing else. Here's the deal, when you read out loud, you're forced to *not* skip the most important part of this book, the Word of God, and hearing your voice, as well as mentally seeing the words, immeasurably cements the words to your very being! [So]... let me implore you, take advantage of this suggestion, and I guarantee you'll be amazed, and much better off for it."

Speaking to "Jewish Christians," Peter sets the stage for the new birth. Here's his short history lesson on the prophecy of Jesus Christ, His purpose and plan of salvation for each of us.

What your about to read, is pure gold!
"Praise to God for a Living Hope"

Praise be to the God and Father of our Lord Jesus Christ! In his great mercy he has given us new birth into a living hope through the resurrection of Jesus Christ from the dead, and into an inheritance that can never perish, spoil or fade—kept in heaven for you, who through faith are shielded by God's power until the coming of the salvation that is ready to be revealed in the last time.

Stop for a minute! Let this sink in. What you have just read in a nutshell, is God's purpose in sending His Son Jesus Christ to this Earth! So now, what do we do about it? *Continuing on...Lets listen in on Peter, as he speaks...*

In this you greatly rejoice, though now for a little while you may have had to suffer grief in all kinds of trials. These have come so that your faith—of greater worth than gold, which perishes even though refined by fire—may be proved genuine and may result in praise, glory and honor when Jesus Christ is revealed. Though you have not seen him, you love him; and even though you do not see him now, you believe in him and are filled with an inexpressible and glorious joy, for you are receiving the goal of your faith, the salvation of your souls.

If you didn't just say, *WOW* to what you've just read, then you're "Wower" is broken! You've just read of the value of "faith," the actual centerpiece of MSM.
The scripture continues...

Concerning this salvation, the prophets, who spoke of the grace that was to come to you, searched intently and with the greatest care, trying to find out the time and circumstances to which the <u>Spirit of Christ</u> in them was pointing when he predicted the sufferings of the Messiah and the glories that would follow. It was revealed to them that they were not serving themselves but you, when they spoke of the things that have now been told you by those who have preached the gospel to you by the Holy Spirit sent from heaven. Even angels long to look into these things.

"Be Holy"

Here are Peter's reasons why you should live a godly life. *Continuing...*

Therefore, prepare your <u>minds for action</u>; be <u>self-controlled</u>; set your hope fully on the grace to be given you when Jesus Christ is revealed. <u>As obedient children</u> do not conform to the evil desires you had when you lived in ignorance. But just as he who called you is holy, so be holy in all you do; for it is written: "<u>Be holy, because I am holy</u>."

Since you call on a Father who judges each man's work impartially, live your lives as strangers here in <u>reverent fear</u>. For you know that it was not with perishable things such as silver or gold that you were redeemed from the empty way of life handed down to you from your forefathers, but with the precious blood of Christ, a lamb

without blemish or defect. He was chosen before the cre-
ation of the world, but was revealed in these last times for
your sake. Through him you believe in God, who raised
him from the dead and glorified him, and so your faith
and hope are in God.

Now that you have purified yourselves by obeying the
truth so that you have sincere love for your brothers, love
one another deeply, from the heart, <u>For you have been</u>
<u>born again, not of perishable seed, but of imperishable,</u>
<u>through the living and enduring word of God</u>. (1 Peter 1:
3–23) (Added emphasis)

Well, if you're like me, you'll need to take the time
and re-read Peter's comments above about the
new birth, the trials you'll experience, the relationship
you will have with God the Father and his Son Jesus
Christ. Then, all of the prophecies of men like Isaiah,
Jeremiah, Job and others who understood what faith
is all about, and how God would send a Savior whose
salvation would be available to all men, not only to the
Jews.

Go ahead...read it again... not the words, but the
meaning of the words. There is a difference. The second
reading will draw you closer to what has been revealed.
I guarantee... you're gonna love it!

Now that you're back... listen to what Titus has to
say about the new child of God.

For the grace of God that brings salvation has appeared
to all men. It teaches us to say "No" to ungodliness and
worldly passions, and to live self-controlled, upright and
godly lives in this present age, while we wait for the
blessed hope—the glorious appearing of our great God
and Savior, Jesus Christ, who gave himself for us to
redeem us from all wickedness and to purify for himself

a people that are his very own, eager to do what is good. (Titus 2:11-14)

With this in mind, speaking of the grace of God which has appeared to all men, including those of Old Testament times... you may have questions about the same Old Testament Covenant that God made with Abraham, and what transpired during that era. These are welcome and needed questions which require biblical answers to verify and confirm the gospel, or what is called the "New Covenant" as it is known. Take note of these following Scriptures, because they provide answers to these potential questions and give confidence in the New Testament Gospel, the New Covenant.

First of all, listen to what Jeremiah has to say, who wrote during Old Testament times, in chapter 31, and then what the writer of Hebrews, in the New Testament has to say about these same Scriptures and their connections to Jesus Christ; the Gospel and the New Covenant.

"The time is coming," declares the LORD, "when I will make a <u>New Covenant</u> with the house of Israel and with the house of Judah. It will not be like the covenant I made with their forefathers when I took them by the hand to lead them out of Egypt, because they broke my covenant, though I was a husband to them," declares the LORD. "This is the covenant I will make with the house of Israel after that time," declares the LORD. "I will put my law in their minds and write it on their hearts. I will be their God, and they will be my people. No longer will a man teach his neighbor, or a man his brother, saying, 'Know the LORD,' because they will all know me, from the least of them to the greatest," declares the LORD. "For I will forgive their wickedness and will remember their sins no more."
(Jeremiah 31:31-34)

Because of this oath, Jesus has become the guarantee of a better covenant.
(Hebrews 7:22)

But the ministry Jesus has received is as superior to theirs as the covenant of which he is mediator is superior to the old one, and it is founded on better promises.
(Hebrews 8:6)

Here are additional scriptural confirmations of the New Birth, or the New Covenant.

I am not ashamed of the gospel, because it is the power of God for the salvation of everyone who believes: first for the Jew, then for the Gentile. (Romans 1:16)

For he says, "In the time of my favor I heard you, and in the day of salvation I helped you." I tell you, now is the time of God's favor, now is the day of salvation. (2 Corinthians 6:2) (Added emphasis)

Now, from the oldest book in the Bible, you'll discover how God spoke to Job... in his spirit, about the reality of an afterlife. It's almost incomprehensible, apart from the power of a righteous God, for someone in Job's position to even consider the opportunity of being with God for eternity. You would think as a man, living in those times, he would know very little about God, to say nothing of His Son Jesus Christ, who didn't show up for hundreds of years later. *Read these words carefully and thoughtfully, for they have power and presence in each one of our lives.*

For God does speak now one way, now another, though man may not perceive it. In a dream, in a vision of the night, when deep sleep falls on men as they slumber in their beds, he may speak in their ears and terrify them with warnings, to turn man from wrongdoing and keep him from pride, to preserve his soul from the pit, his life from perishing by the sword.

Or a man may be chastened on a bed of pain with constant distress in his bones, so that his very being finds food repulsive and his soul loathes the choicest meal. His flesh wastes away to nothing, and his bones, once hidden, now stick out. His soul draws near to the pit and his life to the messengers of death.

"Yet if there is an angel on his side as a mediator, one out of a thousand, to tell a man what is right for him, to be gracious to him and say, 'Spare him from going down to the pit; I have found a ransom for him" then his flesh is renewed like a child's; it is restored as in the days of his youth. He prays to God and finds favor with him. He sees God's face and shouts for joy. He is restored by God to his righteous state.

Then he comes to men and says, 'I sinned, and perverted what was right, but I did not get what I deserved. He redeemed my soul from going down to the pit, and I will live to enjoy the light.' "God does all these things to a man, twice, even three times to turn back his soul from the pit that the light of life may shine on him.(Job 33:14-30) (Added emphasis)

Without a doubt, just as Job knew nothing of what was going on between God and Satan through all of the temptation God allowed Satan to inflict upon him, he still was in touch with God! He knew Him, he believed in Him regardless of all the pain and suffering which he experienced. Think of it, he believed in an eternity with God long before anyone even had inkling that this could be possible.

Now, the Scripture is clear about salvation, including the third person of the Trinity, the Holy Spirit which will occupy your heart and mind providing direction, encouragement, and peace of mind in your world, which is fraught with endless difficulties... difficulties which could get the best of us, if it wasn't for the Holy Spirit calming our spirit and providing enough grace for the day.

And you also were included in Christ when you heard the word of truth, the gospel of your salvation. Having believed, you were marked in Him with a seal, the promised Holy Spirit, who is a deposit guaranteeing our inheritance until the redemption of those who are God's possession—to the praise of his glory.
(Ephesians 1:13-14) (Added emphasis)

You, however, are controlled not by the sinful nature but by the Spirit, if the Spirit of God lives in you. And if anyone does not have the Spirit of Christ, he does not belong to Christ. (Romans 8:9) (Added emphasis)

Don't you know that you yourselves are God's temple and that God's Spirit lives in you? (1 Corinthians 3:16)

May the grace of the Lord Jesus Christ, and the love of God, and the fellowship of the Holy Spirit be with you all. (2 Corinthians 13:14)

Okay, do you remember the story of Nicodemus, the Pharisee, a member of the Jewish ruling council? His story provides us with the final and complete answer God gave to John regarding the New Birth.

Now there was a man of the Pharisees, named Nicodemus, a ruler of the Jews; this man came to Jesus by night and said to Him, "Rabbi, we know that You have come from God as a teacher; for no one can do these signs that You do unless God is with him." Jesus answered and said to him, "Truly, truly, I say to you, unless one is born again he cannot see the kingdom of God." Nicodemus said to Him, "How can a man be born when he is old? He cannot enter a second time into his mother's womb and be born, can he?" Jesus answered, "Truly, truly, I say to you, unless one is born of water and the Spirit he cannot enter into the kingdom of God."That which is born of the flesh is flesh, and that which is born of the Spirit is spirit." Do not be amazed that I said to you, 'You must be born again.' "The wind blows where it wishes and you hear the sound of it, but do not know where it comes from and where it is going; so is everyone who is born of the Spirit."

Nicodemus said to Him, "How can these things be?"

Jesus answered and said to him, "Are you the teacher of Israel and do not understand these things? Truly, truly, I say to you, we speak of what we know and testify of what we have seen, and you do not accept our testimony. If I told you earthly things and you do not believe, how will you believe if I tell you heavenly things? No one has ascended into heaven, but He who descended from heaven: the Son of Man. As Moses lifted up the serpent in the wilderness, even so must the Son of Man be lifted up; so that whoever believes will in Him have eternal life."

"For God so loved the world that He gave His only begotten Son, that whoever believes in Him shall not perish, but have eternal life, for God did not send the Son into the world to judge the world, but that the world might be saved through Him. He who believes in Him is not judged; he who does not believe has been judged already, because he has not believed in the name of the only begotten Son of God. This is the judgment, that the

*Light has come into the world, and men loved the dark-
ness rather than the Light, for their deeds were evil. For
everyone who does evil hates the Light, and does not
come to the Light for fear that his deeds will be exposed.
But he who practices the truth comes to the Light, so that
his deeds may be manifested as having been wrought in
God."*
(John 3:1–21) (NASB) (Added emphasis)

Based on these truths, what is God's simple plan
of salvation for each of us to enjoy the fruits of a new
relationship with God the Father, His Son and His Holy
Spirit of promise? Paul, writing to the Romans made
it indelibly clear as to the plan of God in sending His
Son Jesus to become sin for us. The judgment for our
sin was removed on the cross, when He fulfilled His
Father's plan of redemption for mankind.

Following, is a key part of the 10th chapter of the
book of Romans where Paul demonstrates his compassion for the Jewish nation, or Israelites as he called
them, as well as all non-Jews, or Gentiles as they were
known in this period of history.

After absorbing the words of this chapter, there is no
excuse for any of us, in NOT understanding God's plan
of salvation! This plan is the "New Birth" God speaks
of as your "Second Birth." When reading the powerful
words of this chapter in the book of God, have an open
mind and a willing heart to understand and apply this
to your own life.

Here Paul shares his heart in a very intimate way
with a group of people he loves, and desires the best for
each of them. *Listen, as if he was speaking directly to
you personally...* In truth, He is!

*Brothers, my heart's desire, and prayer to God for the
Israelites are that they may be saved. For I can testify
about them, that they are zealous for God, but their zeal*

is not based on knowledge. Since they did not know the righteousness that comes from God and sought to establish their own, they did not submit to God's righteousness. <u>Christ is the end of the law so that there may be righteousness for everyone who believes</u>.

Moses describes in this way the righteousness that is by the law: "The man who does these things will live by them." But the righteousness that is by faith says: "Do not say in your heart, 'Who will ascend into heaven?' (That is, to bring Christ down) "Or 'Who will descend into the deep?' (That is, to bring Christ up from the dead). But what does it say? "The word is near you; it is in your mouth and in your heart," that is, the word of faith we are proclaiming: <u>That if you confess with your mouth</u>, "<u>Jesus is Lord</u>," <u>and believe in your heart that God raised him from the dead, you will be saved. For it is with your heart that you believe and are justified, and it is with your mouth that you confess and are saved</u>. As the Scripture says, "Anyone who trusts in him will never be put to shame." For there is no difference between Jew and Gentile—the same Lord is Lord of all and richly blesses all who call on him, for, "<u>Everyone who calls on the name of the Lord will be saved</u>." How, then, can they call on the one they have not believed in? And how can they believe in the one of whom they have not heard? And how can they hear without someone preaching to them? And how can they preach unless they are sent? As it is written, "How beautiful are the feet of those who bring good news!"

But not all the Israelites accepted the good news, for Isaiah says; Lord, who has believed our message? <u>Consequently, faith comes from hearing the message, and the message is heard through the Word of Christ</u>. But I ask: Did they not hear? Of course they did: "Their voice has gone out into all the earth, their words to the ends of the world." (Romans 10:1-18) (Added emphasis)

WHAT YOU'VE JUST READ, IS THE PLAN OF GOD FOR YOUR SALVATION. THE CENTERPIECE MESSAGE OF THE ENTIRE BIBLE!

Friends, nothing has changed; there are obstinate people who place more value on their physical life than on their 'never dying' spiritual life.

What is so sad is the apparent misunderstanding of the Truth by many. You don't lose anything by accepting Christ. You gain, because you're not alone anymore! You're not fighting the battle of life by yourself. You now have the God of the Universe dwelling within, prompting and directing your thinking about life. Old useless appetites are replaced by a taste for more understanding, and acknowledgment of God and His Son; Jesus Christ.

Why do people fail to understand this simple truth...? *What's bad is always bad! What's good has never been bad!* Friends, this life is all wrapped up in beautiful packages with colorful ribbons woven in gold thread! We can't wait to break open the box because it just has to be valuable! But, what are we stuck with? Nothing, because the box is empty! The box is our life... it's empty because of deceit, because of sin. What we think is enjoyable, and, may I say, most of the time it is very enjoyable... at least for the moment. But, it isn't long before we are searching once again for something new which will satisfy our never ending search for happiness. At best, everything in a lifetime is temporary, but by now, you know there is something better!

Can you imagine what it could be like to be a new born babe and still know all you know now? To be able to experience the wonderful changes which will take place, changes you once scoffed at and said they were stupid! All because the Spirit of God is real! He is now alive within you... working on helping you to grow up and be a real man or woman. The message is clear.

39

Eternity is in view. A new and exciting perspective on life, seen through a new set of eyes, and is the most precious gift you've ever received! You will never quit thanking God for His gift of love.

This is Imperative #1... "A new belief," or the "Second Birth," and much more could be said; and more Scriptures could be quoted, but let me conclude by saying... What you don't know WILL hurt you, what you do know, based on the above, will eliminate your spiritual death, a death without the presence of God. And, to ensure an everlasting eternity with Him in a place He has prepared for those which love Him.

How about it? Have you applied Gods plan to your life? If you have, seek God in determining how you will be able to put to work what you'll discover in the remaining chapters. There is nothing more exciting than experiencing the opportunity to see a brother or sister, or just an acquaintance, have the light bulb of God turned on in their life!

CHAPTER 2

MSM - Key Imperative #2

A Spirit of Obedience
You disappear and HE takes charge

[*"Having a fully obedient spirit; directed towards God while trusting in his direction for your life."*]
    Second to the salvation decision, is being obedient to God. Anything less, instantly eliminates any credibility for your decision. As it was when you were a child, being obedient, eliminates grief and keeps you out of trouble. Can you think of anyone you should be more obedient to, than God? Always remember this; your faith is measured by your heart of obedience. Contrary to popular opinion, being obedient is not a loss of control. In fact, it's quite the opposite. When a person recognizes their own personal place in life, coming to grips with God's authority, they are now in a position to maximize every aspect of life.

For just as through the disobedience of the one man (Adam) the many were made sinners, so also through the obedience of the one man the many will be made righteous. (Romans 5:19) (Added emphasis)

A s mothers and fathers, there is a common understanding of the word "obedience." As our children
are born into this world, we innately understand how
important it is to teach them the value of being obedient
to us as we teach what is right and wrong, what is good
and bad, what may be hurtful to them and what will be
helpful to them. And... there's the long list of questions
and answers we as parents are faced with, as we rear
our children to the best of our abilities.

To be obedient is to be amenable, compliant, con-
formable, submissive... having a frame of mind which
states this singular truth. None of us have all the
answers. Since this is true, there's a natural hierarchy
to life. We all have a mother and father we are accountable to, or someone we have contracted to work for, or
if you've ever been in the service of your country... obedience to your superiors is #1. Consider the following
simple, but accurate analogy.

As children, when we play sandlot baseball, we choose
up sides and elect someone to be our team leader. The
leader is in charge, and we must be obedient to him or
her. Also, to keep the game honest, we find someone to
umpire the game. Now, both leaders of the two teams,
and the players, are under the control and direction of
the umpire.

With this simple reminder, obedience is as necessary as the food we eat, the sleep we need, the air we
breathe, and most of all... the love we demonstrate, so
most would agree... disobedience is self serving and
wrong. It flies in the face of all that is good.

As Paul the Apostle, in the Scripture above has
stated; Adam's "disobedience" to God, was the beginning of human sin, a disease we have inherited, and for
which there is a daily price we must pay. This disobedience, or Sin, *(better stated,)* was the cause behind the
rule of law. The law from the beginning was God cen-

tered, God provided, and without His law, there would be no <u>knowledge of sin</u>.

This book is not meant to be a treatise on the law, God's Ten Commandments, or the Law of Moses which was man's extension of God's commandments... but only to make clear there is a need for rules and regulations to control the disobedience of man caused by original sin.

Listen to the words of Jesus Christ, in His direct teaching about the law.

The Fulfillment of the Law

Do not think that I have come to abolish the Law or the Prophets; I have not come to abolish them but to fulfill them. I tell you the truth, until heaven and earth disappear, not the smallest letter, not the least stroke of a pen will by any means disappear from the Law until everything is accomplished. Anyone who breaks one of the least of these commandments and teaches others to do the same will be called least in the kingdom of heaven, but whoever practices and teaches these commands will be called great in the kingdom of heaven. For I tell you that unless your righteousness surpasses that of the Pharisees and the teachers of the law, you will certainly not enter the kingdom of heaven.
(Matthew 5:17-20)

Jesus came to fulfill all and to teach His father's ceremonial, civil, and moral laws which were given to help the people of God to more completely love Him, with all of their hearts and minds.

Even a superficial reading of the Old Testament Scripture is enough to understand God's people failed miserably in following these laws, and often misquoted and misapplied them to suit their own purposes. God gave them every opportunity to repent and turn to Him.

Sometimes they listened, but most of the time they didn't.

First, the "Ceremonial Laws" were designed by God to direct Israel in its worship. They were specifically designed to point forward to the time of Jesus Christ, and after Jesus death on the cross and resurrection they were no longer needed.

Secondly, the "Civil Law" applied to day-to-day living in Israel. Much of our common law today stemmed from these very specific rules and regulations which certainly aren't to be applied now, but gave birth to the need for a lawful society instituting certain limitations on the people.

Thirdly, the "Moral Law," or the "Ten Commandments," is still applicable today and reveals the nature and will of God Himself. Jesus obeyed the moral law completely, and sought ways through various stories and parables to direct people back to its original purpose. The truth of what He faced during His lifetime may be summarized in the way the Pharisees had altered these laws into a confusing mass of rules and regulations, which accomplished nothing more than building personal pride in themselves, and not love and devotion for God.

Does this sound familiar? Have you not seen, or even maybe experienced this same kind of legalistic approach to so-called Christian living? It seems mankind today is still blinded by their own importance and power to control the lives of their brothers and sisters in Christ, by requiring conformity to certain church rules which are akin to the Pharisees during the days of Christ.

Question; I wonder how many people have been driven from the church because of pharisaical attitudes and rules of conduct not found in the Holy Scriptures? When these attitudes are present, God is not honored and, on the contrary, Satan is pleased, just as he was with the Pharisees! Also, there is an important contradiction in the use of legalistic, man-made rules and regulations found today in many churches. It's in non-compliance with God's direct admonition against personal judgment.

Here's what Paul, being led by the Holy Spirit of God, had to say on this subject . . .

Therefore let us stop passing judgment on one another. Instead, make up your mind not to put any stumbling block or obstacle in your brother's way. (Romans 14:13)

Example: Rules of conduct and dress codes not found in the Holy Scriptures, have been added over the years by many churches, in an attempt to define "godliness" like the Pharisees of Jesus time. Even to the extent of judging the methods Jesus used, and ultimately playing a role in bringing Him to the cross.

Let me be clear, a large part of our sinful nature, falls under the heading of judgmental-ism. We find ourselves trying to control our church culture, by seeking to define what holiness is all about. Example; In days gone by, a woman, to be godly, was made to believe it is sinful to wear long slacks, or the habit of smoking cigarettes or going to movies is patently wrong, and is a direct indication of a person's "worldliness." That judgmental-ism has subsided to a degree, and has been replaced in some churches by a distain for up-beat Praise music in the church, where certain musical instruments are patently sinful, or "worldly." These would include in particular, drum sets, guitars and other instruments not found in churches of the past.

Then, there's the concern by church leadership about not up-setting the older crowd for fear of the un-spoken concern in losing their weekly Tithe. This being true, how should the church view these realities of church life?

First of all, we must make sure we don't fit the description of what Jesus, in the book of Matthew, called a Hypocrite: *"Woe to you, teachers of the law and Pharisees, you hypocrites! <u>You are like whitewashed tombs</u>, which look beautiful on the outside but on the inside are full of the bones of the dead and everything unclean. (Matthew 23:27) (Added emphasis)*

In fact, in the whole 23rd chapter of Matthew, Jesus is condemning this sinful use of hypocrisy in the church. What's the answer...? Just don't get caught up in religious hypocrisy! Focus on doing what is pleasing to God. If it means preaching against some un-Godly attitude based solely on preference, and not on actual merit in the presentation of the Word of God, either in preaching, or in music...<u>fearlessly preach against it</u>! God's in control of the outcome. Too many times, our actions stem from our own fears and concerns about those things which only God can control. Forget the potential loss of Tithes and offerings...preach the truth, and God will supply! The people of the church seek truth, that's why they're there.

So, May I submit to you, all of these things of cultural origin, must be judged by the individual, as he or she, seeks conformity of their lives to God's Word? Then, their own personal testimony of the change which has occurred in their life direction after receiving Jesus Christ into their heart is between them and God, and no one else, including the church they attend. The church should not attempt, in any way, to teach anything not found in the written Word of God. It is certainly true that the Word of God teaches principles of living, but it's not the job of the church to define those principles in specific legalistic terms.

Our "obedience" is to God and God alone. Not the church, not a list of written or unwritten rules by the church of certain sins they deem worldly, as it were, but only to God and His Word which was written for indi-

46

viduals to understand and live by. If, on the other hand, a person is selected to serve the church in a Biblical category such as pastor, or bishop, or deacon, then the Scripture is clear concerning qualifications which must be met by the individual to perform this service. These stated qualifications should be the norm for all of us as we serve Him.

Jesus actions and teachings centered on His obedience to His Father, and was the basis for all of the teaching in the New Testament. The reality of His life was the fulfillment and purpose of all Old Testament Scripture from the very beginning of time until the time of John the Baptist in his introduction of Jesus Christ as the Messiah! Now, how does the obedience of Jesus affect our lives?

This thing of obedience and disobedience is the result of God providing man with "Free Choice." God allowed Adam the choice to be obedient to Him regarding "eating of the fruit of the tree of Good and Evil."

Understand this truth, deceit is powerful! It is the final definition of sin. Adam and Eve were both guilty of falling prey to this deceit. They had the opportunity and choice to do otherwise, but they made the wrong decision.

All of the above is because of the very "Essence of God," and this essence is wrapped up in the following statement.

"God is Love, and Love without Freedom is not Love."

Let's take another look at the Scripture above...

For just as through the disobedience of the one man (Adam) the many were made sinners, so also through the obedience of the one man (Jesus Christ) the many will be made righteous. (Romans 5:19) (Added emphasis)

Paul emphatically states the truth of Jesus' obedience to His father... God!

Jesus Christ, the second person of the Holy Trinity was sent by the Father to be the payment for our sins, that is, for our deceit and for our disobedience. Because of His Holy Love for each of His children, He stood before the judge of heaven, His Father, and was willing to capture the sin of the entire world into His very being. The totality of that sin was from the very beginning of each life lived on this planet to the very end of their life... That is... past, present, and future sin to be forever forgotten by God Himself when each person is willing to be "obedient" to God the Father, by accepting Jesus Christ into their heart and life, how; by simple faith in the grace and love of God. This was made possible through the death on the cross, and the resurrection of His Son, Jesus Christ!

Additionally, obedience is not something extra we do, it is our daily duty.

"Suppose one of you had a servant plowing or looking after the sheep. Would he say to the servant when he comes in from the field, Come along now and sit down to eat'? Would he not rather say, Prepare my supper, get yourself ready and wait on me while I eat and drink; after that you may eat and drink'? Would he thank the servant because he did what he was told to do? You also, when you have done everything you were told to do, should say, 'we are unworthy servants; we have only done our duty.'" (Luke 17:7-10)

Then, we see the faith of the "lepers." They obeyed God and went to the priest to have their leprosy proclaimed clean. They believed God and were cleansed while on their way, in obedience to the Lord. Catch the power of "obedience" in this short, but powerful verse from the word of God

When he saw them, he said, "Go, show yourselves to the priests." And as they went, they were cleansed. (Luke 17:14)

Being "blind" to the truth of God's Word is like trying to see clearly without your glasses. Everything is out of focus causing you to stumble. You look for guidance in all the wrong places. When you finally decide to seek "truth," you'll be given a new set of glasses. You'll begin to "see" like never before. Truth will now become "sacred" to you.

Do you remember the story of the "blind man" who received sight by being obedient? Here's the story . . .

As he went along, he saw a man blind from birth. His disciples asked him, "Rabbi, who sinned, this man, or his parents that he was born blind?"

"Neither this man nor his parents sinned," said Jesus, "but this happened so that the work of God might be displayed in his life. As long as it is day, we must do the work of him who sent me. Night is coming, when no one can work. While I am in the world, I am the light of the world."

Having said this, he spit on the ground, made some mud with the saliva, and put it on the man's eyes. "Go," he told him, "wash in the Pool of Siloam" (this word means Sent). So the man went and washed, and came home seeing.

His neighbors and those who had formerly seen him begging asked. "Isn't this the same man who used to sit and

beg?" Some claimed that he was. Others said, "No, he only looks like him." But he himself insisted, "I am the man."

"How then were your eyes opened?" they demanded.

He replied, "The man they call Jesus made some mud and put it on my eyes. He told me to go to Siloam and wash. So I went and washed, and then I could see." "Where is this man?" they asked him. "I don't know," he said.

They brought to the Pharisees the man who had been blind. Now the day on which Jesus had made the mud and opened the man's eyes was a Sabbath. Therefore the Pharisees also asked him how he had received his sight. "He put mud on my eyes," the man replied, "and I washed, and now I see." (John 9:1-15) (Added emphasis)

To know, love and cherish the very Son of God requires the simplicity of obedience. That is, being "obedient" to His plan and purpose for your life.

Taste and see that the LORD is good; blessed is the man who takes refuge in him. (Psalm 34:8)

Here we see the words of David, after pretending to be insane so that he could escape from the evil king Achish.

Refuge in God is an invitation to obedience. As a new child of God, there is much to learn. There will be times of obedience and disobedience on your part. But, the important thing is now you will be able to distinguish between the two. Before entering into this relationship with God, life was different. It was left up to you to determine good from bad, right from wrong, and to be in state of constant wonderment about the proper path to follow. Usually, the judgment was made on how much money I can make going this way instead of that way. Now, to realize the focus on money has become secondary, or maybe even further down the ladder, since you've come to understand that God is the provider of all things.

There are additional things to consider on the subject of "Obedience." James, in the story he tells below, provides for us a ton of reasons to not be in disagreement with this God ordained plan for living. A plan which, when followed will insure against creating heartache, pain and suffering for others. It will, if followed, insure just the opposite!

My dear brothers, take note of this: Everyone should be quick to listen, slow to speak and slow to become angry, for man's anger does not bring about the righteous life that God desires. Therefore, get rid of all moral filth and the evil that is so prevalent and humbly accept the word planted in you, which can save you.

Do not merely listen to the word, and so deceive yourselves. Do what it says. Anyone who listens to the word but does not do what it says is like a man who looks at his face in a mirror and, after looking at himself, goes away and immediately forgets what he looks like. But the man who looks intently into the perfect law that gives freedom, and <u>continues to do this</u>, not forgetting what he has heard, <u>but doing it</u>—he will be blessed in what he does.

If anyone considers himself religious and yet does not keep a tight rein on his tongue, he deceives himself and his religion is worthless. Religion that God our Father accepts as pure and faultless is this: to look after orphans and widows in their distress and to keep oneself from being polluted by the world.
(James 1:19-27) (Added emphasis)

Finally, listen to the following Scripture as we see the direct command of Jesus to his followers.

Jesus replied, "Foxes have holes and birds of the air have nests, but the Son of Man has no place to lay his head." Another disciple said to him, "Lord, first let me go and bury my father." But Jesus told him, "follow me, and let the dead bury their own dead." (Matthew 8:21-22)

These two verses in Matthew demonstrate the direct command Jesus had with those He selected to be one of His followers. He made it clear there would be great sacrifice and high cost. He demanded complete loyalty with no strings attached. They knew of His complete power over everything. They saw Him in action and they knew with one word, or a single touch He healed those of faith. With the above in mind, they knew that nothing should take precedence over following Him.

In the book of James we quickly learn that believing is not enough...

You believe that there is one God. Good! Even the demons believe that–and shudder. (James 2:19)

Satan's demons believed and knew that Jesus had power over them and that He was the Son of God. *(Matthew 8:29)* "Faith is more than belief alone." This was the central plot and purpose of the writing of the book of James. When you study this book, you will soon learn that we are to live out our faith by obeying his commands. Commands are "actions." It is the day to day living out of our faith, in complete obedience to Him.

Godly Obedience, a short Definition

Obedience is the act of "acting" on the promptings from God, "The Holy Spirit." There is no pausing, no questioning, and no attempt to rationalize the "action" away. No inward rebellion or the making of an excuse to say no.

It's by His powerful faith He has placed in us, to put feet, hands, and hearts in gear immediately, and to step on the gas pedal all the way to the floor! He will steer us to the goal! He will tell us when to put on the brakes, He will open the door allowing us to step into His presence and view the glory of what He has prepared for us! And, we should never — never take credit for the results of acting on a prompting from Him. Remember... Never!

Obedience then, is ... a gift from God!

CHAPTER 3

MSM - Key Imperative #3

A Seeking Heart

A thirst for Truth

[*"Having a seeking heart which is fully open to His promptings and nudgings for specific life directions,"*]

A seeking heart is different than a willing heart. When the Holy Spirit draws a person to Jesus Christ and that person ultimately accepts the Lord as their Savior, they had to be "willing" to do so. On the other hand, after you've made this wonderful decision, it's imperative that you have a desire to continue to "seek first the Kingdom of God."

Matthew Chapter 6 is speaking directly to the recently born again believer in Jesus Christ. Here, Matthew was dealing with a number of subjects, not the least of which was the subject of worry. A natural tendency, born out of fear, or concern for what other people may think, or simply the result of not walking close to God. As a newborn babe in Christ, this was to be expected and was purely natural.

Here's what Matthew had to say about a "seeking heart."

Therefore I tell you, do not worry about your life, what you will eat or drink; or about your body, what you will wear. Is not life more important than food, and the body more important than clothes? Look at the birds of the air; they do not sow or reap or store away in barns, and yet your heavenly Father feeds them. Are you not much more valuable than they? Who of you by worrying can add a single hour to his life? And why do you worry about clothes? See how the lilies of the field grow. They do not labor or spin. Yet I tell you that not even Solomon in all his splendor was dressed like one of these. If that is how God clothes the grass of the field, which is here today and tomorrow is thrown into the fire, will he not much more clothe you, O you of little faith? So do not worry, saying, 'What shall we eat?' or 'What shall we drink?' or 'What shall we wear?' For the pagans run after all these things, and your heavenly Father knows that you need them. But seek first His kingdom and His righteousness, and all these things will be given to you as well. Therefore do not worry about tomorrow, for tomorrow will worry about itself. Each day has enough trouble of its own. (Matthew 6:25-34)

Touché Touché

In the Old testament, in the second book of Chronicles, there was a number of instances where seeking the Lord," was an imperative in the lives of the Israelites.

Those from every tribe of Israel who set their hearts on seeking the LORD, the God of Israel, followed the Levites to Jerusalem to offer sacrifices to the LORD, the God of their Fathers. (2 Chronicles 11:16)

The Bible is clear about the need for us to seek the Lord with a willing heart, a heart of desire and expectation for knowing Him personally, by the study of His Word the Bible, and then through prayer... seeking His approval on the decisions of life.

Listen again to what Matthew has to say concerning seeking God through prayer:

And when you pray, do not be like the hypocrites, for they love to pray standing in the synagogues and on the street corners to be seen by men. I tell you the truth they have received their reward in full. But when you pray, go into your room, close the door and pray to your Father, who is unseen. Then your Father, who sees what is done in secret, will reward you. And when you pray, do not keep on babbling like pagans, for they think they will be heard because of their many words. Do not be like them, for your Father knows what you need before you ask him. (Matthew 6:5-8)

Listen to what Timothy has to say about studying the Word of God as a way of seeking Him.

<u>*Study to show thyself approved unto God*</u>*, a workman that needeth not to be ashamed, rightly dividing the word of truth. (2 Timothy 2:15) (KJV) (Added emphasis)*

Pause with me for a moment, as we continue to consider "Seeking God" as a major Imperative of MSM.

You need to think of it this way . . . "Faith," the very essence of MSM is a "Mind-Set" which expects God to take action on our behalf. When we accept this premise and concept, and then take action, our fears are overcome, and in their place there is peace and joy! Why? Because we take Jesus at His word, and here's what He has to say in the book of Matthew.

"Ask and it will be given to you; seek and you will find; knock and the door will be opened to you. For everyone who asks receives; he who seeks finds; and to him who knocks, the door will be opened." (Matthew 7:7-8)

In this Scripture, Jesus is simply making sure we understand since we are His children, He will answer our requests just the same as we answer the requests of our own children. Just as there are qualifications in what we provide our own children, there are also qualifications and how God answers our prayers, but, we are to make our requests known to Him in believing faith that He will answer them according to his will. Whether we get what we want, and ask for, is another question, not unlike how we respond to our children's requests.

Matthew speaks to us the words of Jesus in amplification of the above truth.

"Which of you, if his son asks for bread, will give him a stone? Or if he asks for a fish, will give him a snake? If you, then, though you are evil, know how to give good gifts to your children, how much more will your Father in heaven give good gifts to those who ask him?" So in everything, do to others what you would have them do to you, for this sums up the Law and the Prophets. (Matthew 7:9-12)

The essence of what Jesus is saying is; pursue me with your desires and heartfelt needs, and don't ever give up! When we give up, we are really saying to ourselves and to God, for that matter, *"I didn't believe you were going to give it to me anyhow."* This kind of attitude is not faith. It's nothing but a pre-determined outcome, based on our own personal judgment of the situation. When this attitude is present, you're simply wasting your time and God's time as well, when you pray. In fact, God does not listen to those kinds of prayers that emanate from an unbelieving heart because it's not a heart driven by faith in God.

So, whenever you pray with a predetermined presumption of the outcome, you are really removing yourself from the very presence of God! What could be worse than that?

Here's Webster's definition of the verb, "seeking;" . . . *to make a search for.* Therefore, seeking or searching is synonymous. This being true, what does the Bible tell us we should be doing as Christians on a regular basis? Well, listen to what Jesus had to say to the unbelieving religious leaders.

Search the scriptures; for in them ye think ye have eternal life: and they are they which testify of me. (John 5:39) (KJV) (Added emphasis)

Many of these religious leaders were fully aware of what the Bible taught concerning the coming of the Messiah, but failed to apply what they learned to their own lives. They knew the scriptures pointed to His coming, but they had no desire to connect the dots! They were entrenched in their own religious beliefs, as long as they didn't interfere with what THEY wanted to believe.

How true that scenario is today! But again, we have a choice. We can continue through life just the way we are, or we can search the Scriptures and quickly learn that Jesus Christ was who He said He was. Read the Scripture once again, and be careful not to miss the last part of the verse.

Search the scriptures; for in them ye think ye have eternal life: and they are they which testify of me. (Added emphasis)

Metaphorically, to search the Scriptures is to "Google God!"

In the Book of Luke, Jesus tells His disciples a very poignant story.

Then he said to them, "Suppose one of you has a friend, and he goes to him at midnight and says, 'Friend, lend me three loaves of bread, because a friend of mine on a journey has come to me, and I have nothing to set before him.' "

"Then the one inside answers, 'Don't bother me. The door is already locked, and my children are with me in bed. I can't get up and give you anything.' I tell you, though he will not get up and give him the bread because he is his friend, yet because of the man's boldness he will get up and give him as much as he needs.' "
(Luke 11:5-8)

God expects us to be bold in our seeking of Him. He expects us to be bold when we come to Him in prayer seeking the help only He can provide. As He continues the story, Jesus makes it abundantly clear to His disciples this reality, and to us as well. He loves us, and because of His love for us, He will give us the desires of our heart as long as we are seeking Him with proper purposes in mind; purposes which are not centered on our own selfish interests and desires.

"So I say to you: Ask and it will be given to you; seek and you will find; knock and the door will be opened to you. For everyone who asks receives; he who seeks finds; and to him who knocks, the door will be opened.
(Luke11:9-10)

When an individual bows his heart and mind to Jesus Christ and accepts the biblical account of His life, death and resurrection in payment for their sins, and is now a child of God, he or she not only will experience the redeeming power which can only be supplied by the God of the universe, but will now witness the magnificent power of prayer and the promise Jesus has made to each one of His children to answer those godly prayers.

You will personally witness the power of God on your life as he provides for you and those you are concerned about, when you seek Him in faith believing.

The many life experiences you've read in MSM are a personal testimony to this truth. And, may I say... there are hundreds and hundreds of more specific situations where the power of God took charge and made a difference when nothing else could.

Now, the following in-depth look at what God sees buried within our very being... an honest desire to please Him, or, could it be a phony walk with Him in order to please others and gain their acceptance.

Which is it?

CHAPTER 4

MSM – Key Imperative #4

A Desire to Demonstrate Faith
Love takes over in spades

[Now that you have a basic understanding of salvation, the new belief, along with knowing the importance of being "obedient to God" and then also having a "seeking heart" to know more about Him, life now is simply "living the Christian life."]

It can become very easy to say I have a desire to please him by demonstrating my faith, and there are many so-called Christians, if asked that question, would rattle off a long list of things they've done throughout their life, which in their judgment, should have been pleasing to the Lord. Well, you could say... sort of an attempt in justifying their outward relationship with the Lord.

Since we have no business judging others, then this thing of "loving God," is simply a "personal heart matter." No one will ever know how much you please God, because no one knows what's in your heart. Only God knows! The main reason this is true, is because it is impossible to judge another person's motives. We can look at outward appearances, and conclude a person is walking close with the Lord, or may fall into the category of what we call a "nominal Christian." Personally, I believe we spend way too much time making judgments and comparisons about other people and their walk with the Lord, and do so to make ourselves look better in the eyes of God. This is simply childish and an indication of immaturity in the child of God.

Speaking of childish... I just have to throw this in here.

The entire hubbub we're now undergoing in this country about President Obama and his personal view of religion, whether Christian or Muslim is nothing more than a waste of time. Obviously, it's all about politics, and has little to do with his relationship to God or for that matter to Allah. For the moment, I will assume you understand there is a distinct difference between the two. As the Bible teaches, there is only one God, and that God is not the God of Mohamed, called Allah.

So, that said, how do we please God, and how can we measure our personal desire to do so?

First of all, if we know we have been truly saved by the power of the gospel, then we must put our "Obedience to God" as the number one consideration above everything else that we do or think about in life.

God must be #1! That is, before everything else we may think of, such as; making a living, the food we eat, the clothes we wear, the pleasures of life, and even the concern we have for others. Above all else . . . God must be #1!

Secondly, we must be devoted to the study of the Word of God. Here is a powerful admonition in seeking to educate ourselves on a consistent daily basis.

Do your best to present yourself to God as one approved, a workman who does not need to be ashamed and who correctly handles the word of truth.
(2 Timothy 2:15)

If you're having problems studying the Word of God, it's high time you take inventory by answering yourself, and your heart of hearts, as to why you're having difficulty in studying the Bible. Consider the following simple reality.

In order to be strong physically, your body requires the intake of food on a regular daily basis, and God has provided us with an appetite in order to exist for a lifetime. From a healthy spiritual perspective, God has also provided each new child of God a new healthy appetite for the Word of God.

Notice, I said... each new child of God. If you are not yet a Born again Believer, you most likely do not have an appetite for the study of the Bible.

When the Holy Spirit of God enters into your life, you will automatically experience a joy and love for the Word of God! It is unmistakable. It is totally different than reading just any other book written by the best author you can think of. And, it is not just "reading the book." You'll find a new excitement in "studying" the lives of the various people who lived prior to the coming of the Lord Jesus Christ. You'll begin to understand answers to many of your questions. You'll begin to understand the plan of God from the very beginning of time, until this present time. You'll begin to understand the essence of God's Word, His Scripture, as he enlightens you about every aspect of life you'll ever think about.

If you're missing this appetite; if you could care less about the Bible, and yet you claim to be a child of God, you may be knowingly or unknowingly, playing games with yourself about your honest belief in Jesus Christ as your own personal Lord and Savior! Let me tell you friend, you are walking on scary ground! There are biblical stories, like Ananias and his wife, Sapphira . . . who together, spent more time thinking about themselves, than thinking about their relationship with God. If you remember the story, God took their lives that day, because of their lies concerning the sale of property and keeping some of the money for themselves, while indicating otherwise. But, the Apostle Peter knew better. Follow the story...

Now a man named Ananias, together with his wife Sapphira, also sold a piece of property. With his wife's full knowledge he kept back part of the money for himself, but brought the rest and put it at the apostles' feet.

Peter said, "Ananias, how is it that Satan has so filled your heart that you have lied to the Holy Spirit and have kept for yourself some of the money you received for the land? Didn't it belong to you before it was sold? And after it was sold, wasn't the money at your disposal? What made you think of doing such a thing? You have not lied to men but to God."

When Ananias heard this, he fell down and died. And great fear seized all who heard what had happened. Then the young men came forward, wrapped up his body, and carried him out and buried him.

About three hours later his wife came in, not knowing what had happened. Peter asked her, "Tell me, is this the price you and Ananias got for the land?" "Yes," she said, "That is the price." Peter said to her, "How could you agree to test the Spirit of the Lord? Look! The feet of the men who buried your husband are at the door, and they will carry you out also."

At that moment she fell down at his feet and died. Then the young men came in and, finding her, carried her out and buried her beside her husband. Great fear seized the whole church and all who heard about these events. (Acts 5:1-11)

As Christians, we of all people, need to live a life full of integrity, full of honesty, and filled with desire to please the Lord in all we do, especially concerning our relationship with Him. There is a secret for pleasing God and enjoying His joy and happiness in doing so. Listen in your heart of hearts, as Paul describes just what this is all about!

Therefore, as God's chosen people, holy and dearly loved, clothe yourselves with compassion, kindness, humility, gentleness and patience. Bear with each other and <u>for-give whatever grievances you may have against one another. Forgive as the Lord forgave you</u>. And over all these virtues put on love, which binds them all together in perfect unity.

Let the peace of Christ rule in your hearts, since as members of one body you were called to peace. And be thankful. Let the word of Christ dwell in you richly as you teach and admonish one another with all wisdom, and as you sing psalms, hymns and spiritual songs with gratitude in your hearts to God. And whatever you do, whether in word or deed, do it all in the name of the Lord Jesus, giving thanks to God the Father through him. (Colossians 3:12-17) (Added emphasis)

Could it be that you are chained, literally chained by a lack of forgiveness? Oftentimes when this is true, people are not even aware of it. They have hate in their hearts for others because of what has happened to them. Underneath it all, they seek freedom from the constant reminders of their past, but they do not have a clue of what they are able to accomplish to gain freedom.

In seeking to please God by asking for His forgiveness when you made the choice to repent of your sins and ask Him to be your Lord and Master, you fully expected Him to forgive you didn't you? Well, to please Him, you need to obediently begin making a list, either in your mind or even on paper of those people you have hurt in one way or another, or those which have hurt you along the way. You need to name them! And then something very important... separate the individual, from the offense in your mind.

The next step is to speak to God in prayer indicating your desire to forgive those who have hurt you and to ask God to remove the memory of this difficulty from your mind. In fact, as a newborn Christian you now have the opportunity and even the responsibility to pray for those who have hurt you. How about those people you may have hurt yourself? You need to go through the same process outlined above, asking forgiveness in each individual case from God, and then to communicate with those people individually seeking their forgiveness. It's not good enough just to say "I'm sorry." The reason this is not good enough, is because it's nothing more than a one-sided admission of guilt. What needs to be done is to; "Ask for their Forgiveness!" Their agreement to your request is like receiving a receipt for a paid up debt. Bottom line, when God forgives us we must be willing to forgive others, and when we forgive them we need to go to them in the same manner as mentioned above, and tell them about what God has done for us and how important it is to let them know you have forgiven them. Don't be surprised when you take this God driven step, what you have done may affect their lives for eternity.

Finally, to gain the freedom and cleansing of pain and hurt from your heart and mind, you must forgive yourself! Stop and think about it. Most, if not all of us, are disgusted with some of the things we've said or done in the past, things which have caused much pain and suffering because of personal guilt. If you've accepted Christ as savior, these actions and thoughts have already been forgiven by God. But, we hang on to them for some reason. Here's the action necessary. Just tell yourself the truth! Ask yourself for forgiveness by claiming the promise of God. Admit to yourself a known sin you've accomplished against yourself. No, that's not a crazy statement. It's the truth. It's possible to sin in this way, by misguided faulty belief about your weaknesses or judgments or your thinking processes in the past. STOP, ask yourself for forgiveness. In doing so, you are asking God to remove that history from your mind, and to free up your heart.

Forgiveness is the Essence of pleasing God!

Part 2

Speaking Out Courageously
Acting on God Inspired
Direction
Pray without Ceasing

"Action Time"

God's Workplace

The following three Key Imperatives will pinpoint God's expectations for each one of us as we seek to serve Him in whatever area of service he has called us to. It's not unlike the college graduate who has just completed the needed instruction required to accomplish his or her future goals. Now it's time to put all of that learning to work by acting on the basic instruction received.

The student soon learns what they have just spent thousands of dollars to attain, is just the beginning of their understanding of how incomplete their education really is.

The first four "Key Imperatives" provided the believer in Jesus Christ with a platform of understanding, allowing them the ability to go to work for God. Just like the graduating student, who can't hardly wait until they get their first job, and are now able to begin to make sense of all they've learned. So now... the remaining three "Key Imperatives" define the *"workplace"* of the new Christian, a place where both God and you have the opportunity to test each other. *"God... in providing His provision for you, and you... in seeking to learn the landscape of service by depending upon His promises; answers to prayers; nudging, and finally, to participate in the many miracles He wants you to deliver."* MMSM

It was exciting when you graduated from college, and the anticipation of finding that first new job was worth it all! The new job would be a way to put all you've learned to work, to see how realistic your education really was when it came time to receive your payoff... Question: *"Was what you could earn from the new job worth it all?"*

This is where the similarity ends. The spiritual payoff we receive in serving God, will never be known in this life; apart from the human satisfaction in knowing God has used you as an instrument of His saving grace, in the lives of all of the people He has led you to, and you have responded by being faithful and truthful to His word.

There is nothing in this life that can compare to the results gained by being obedient to the Word of God. No amount of money, no amount of temporal satisfaction, no amount of power... Absolutely NOTHING can compare to the opportunity each one of us has in helping others to attain eternal salvation with God.

Therefore, do not gloss over the importance of these three remaining "Key Imperatives." In fact, take what you read here, and expand upon it in your study of God's Word to help you personalize just what you should be doing for Him.

CHAPTER 5

MSM – Key Imperative #5

A Courageous Willingness to Speak out

Fear is a thing of the past

[*"Always be prepared to give an answer to everyone who asks you, and to give the reason for the hope that you have. But do this with gentleness and respect."*] *(1 Peter 3:15)*

Okay, so how do I speak out courageously, you may ask?

In light of the many "kooks" that are out there in our world infecting almost every part of our society, there certainly is a reticence in being a witness in the world for Christianity. *No one wants to purposely take any action that would categorize them as a kook!*

Before commenting on this, allow me to ask this all important question.

Is it a copout when you place Christianity into the world of kookiness?

Since one of the key tenets of Christianity is honesty, then I believe anyone with an ounce of it would have to agree... if in fact they've studied it, that Christianity is the only "solid basis" by which we have the opportunity to understand what life is all about, where it started, and where it will end.

The God of this Universe is not complacent. He is sovereign, and holds the keys to all "matter and life" in the Universe; in Heaven; and in particularly on this earth. He is the God of action! He invented it!

So, who's in control here? Is it you? Or, is it your maker, the Lord Jesus Christ... God Himself in the flesh, and now in Heaven.

Remember, I'm speaking to you as a Christian, a person who has named the name of Jesus Christ as their Lord and Savior, and yet many fail to live up to His commands. "Listen to this particular command, and come to grips with the personal nature of this message." Don't continue to avoid it, for if you do, you will certainly suffer loss both here in this world, and in the world to come... Heaven! *Here it is...*

He said to them, "Go into all the world and preach the good news to all creation." (Mark 16:15)

So, you may ask, "how do I preach the gospel, I'm not a preacher!" My response...as a newborn Christian, yes you are! Webster's dictionary makes it very clear... Preach; *"To urge or advocate earnestly."* In plain English it simply means *"to make known!"*

That was easy enough, but I fully understand where most people come from as they consider the word "preacher." Allow me to explain...

There is an unwarranted attitude towards the word "preaching"...being overly forceful, demanding, I'm right-you're wrong, I have all the answers, and on it goes. But I'm here to tell you, when Mark used this word to describe the words of Jesus to His disciples, it was none of the above. On the contrary, Jesus just wanted all of us to do exactly as he did, and *that was* to simply share; as I'm trying to do in this book, the truth of the good news... the "Gospel" of our Lord and Savior Jesus Christ, to everyone whom Jesus prompts us to communicate. There are many ways to deliver the message; that, my friend, is "preaching."

In no way is it any different than how you share all of those other things you believe in, in a conversational way, and not any different maybe, except for the subject matter. Someone has said, *(A copout I might add)... "Never discuss religion or politics."* Well, if ever there were a time people are talking about politics it's now! And there's a significant reason for that. The overwhelming reason is centered on "the fear of loss," the loss of freedom, the loss of money, even the loss of their homeland to a political power never before encountered in this country, the good 'ole US of A. So, when push comes to shove, complacency begins to lose its foothold in the minds and hearts of people. It's replaced by a new fervor, a new desire to participate and to be counted. People begin doing things they never thought they would do in the name of "freedom!" This is good, and it's what should be happening when we are faced with important decisions in life.

If Christian people would exercise the same fervor in sharing the good news of the Word of God to people in need, there would be a magnificent uprising, or revival in the church, and the world for that matter, not unlike what happened in England many years ago or even in the early days of our country. When we keep to ourselves, go to church on Sunday, do our work whatever it may be, without any thought for others concerning their relationship with God, do you think this is pleasing to Him? Doesn't this fly in the face of His command for us to be obedient to His Word?

Preach the Word; be prepared in season and out of season; correct, rebuke and encourage—with great patience and careful instruction. (2 Timothy 4:2)

Paul said to Timothy... go out into the world and preach! How this is accomplished in your life is between you and God. The verse above essentially states; "Be prepared every day to encourage, helping to show people what God's Word says about how they ought to live their lives." This is His way of rebuking others, not in the sense that we consider rebuking. So, how should we do it...? Do it with patience and careful instruction. The Lord, through Paul, couldn't have been clearer in what he wants us to do. That's each one of us, not just a few, but all of us!

Question; Have there been times when you have spoken out courageously about something you deeply believe in, not necessarily about the Word of God, but something that was really important to you? It wasn't that hard, was it?

Friends, we are all without excuse. If you've read MSM, you should remember my saying that it's only "difficult" the first time. Once you've shared your heart, *(all that's really necessary)* once you've done that, the result is a satisfaction beyond anything you can imagine. Once you've accomplished this, you will not believe how stimulated you are to continue, to purposely look for opportunities to do it over and over again.

Whether you believe it or not, underneath it all, people are hurting, and most need help. When we encounter someone God prompts us speak to about Him, we have no idea what their past experience is concerning the things of God. Generally, we believe we will be rejected out of hand. I'm here to tell you, this kind of situation is more abnormal than not. If the person realizes your attitude is "honest concern" for them, they will usually open up, and begin to listen.

Here's a truth worth considering; no doubt, many people are headed for destruction. The Bible is very clear on this reality. I believe, most times it's not out of stubbornness, but it's nothing more than "thoughtlessness!" It's our job to help them to "stop and think" about where their lives are headed, and then to point out the consequences of ignoring Christ's teaching about salvation. How you can accomplish this is not difficult. The first thing that's required is to be motivated by the command of God, spoken about above.

Here's where it gets interesting. *God wants to speak to them through you...* you're nothing but a male or female messenger! God only wants you to get their attention and then to let Him speak. Here's what I mean by that.

William Fay, the author of... "Share Jesus without Fear," has shared his faith with more than 25,000 people on a one-to-one basis, and provides in his book a clear understanding of how simple it can be to talk to people about the Lord. The basic concept is centered on asking a few simple questions and then to let the Word of God speak and answer each one of those questions.

The concept plan is to "get out of the way" and let God do the convincing through the Holy Spirit. A new relationship with God cannot be sold! It cannot be forced, and it certainly cannot be bought. No amount of giving to the church, and no amount of convincing on our part will get the job done.

I cannot recommend more highly, this wonderful and practical book which provides the necessary tools to become one of God's choice servants in sharing the word of God. "Share Jesus without Fear"[1]

To simply give you a small taste of what Bill Fay has learned from the Word of God, and practiced for many years... here, in a "nutshell" is his concept.

He typically asks five individual questions in a very conversational way. He gets their okay with something like this... *"Hey john, we've talked a little in the past* about life in general, so, do you mind if I ask you a few questions? Don't worry I'm not going to drill you on anything. In fact, I'm not even going to answer them myself! If John says OK, then he proceeds with the following, allowing for sufficient time for the individual to share their answers, and he suggests we do the same.

OPENING QUESTIONS

1. Do you have any kind of spiritual belief?
2. To you, who is Jesus?
3. Do you believe there is a heaven and hell?
4. If you died right now where would you go? If Heaven, why?
5. If what you believe were not true, would you want to know it?

If the person says yes to #5, after answering the previous four questions, then open your Bible, and this is key! *Ask the person to read each of the following Scriptures out loud.*

1. Romans 3:23
   For all have sinned and fall short of the glory of God.
2. Romans 6:23
   For the wages of sin is death, but the gift of God is eternal life in Christ Jesus our Lord.
3. John 3:3
   In reply Jesus declared, "I tell you the truth, no one can see the kingdom of God unless he is born again."

Then ask... "Why do you think Jesus come to die...?" *(Here's your answer;)* "Let's see what the Bible says"....

> *Jesus answered, "I am the way and the truth and the life. No one comes to the Father except through me." (John 14:6)*

4. Romans 10:9-11
   That if you confess with your mouth, "Jesus is Lord," and believe in your heart that God raised him from the dead, you will be saved. For it is with your heart that you believe and are justified, and it is with your mouth that you confess and are saved. As the Scripture says, "Anyone who trusts in him will never be put to shame."

5. 2 Corinthians 5:15
   And he died for all, that those who live should no longer live for themselves but for him who died for them and was raised again.
   Here I am! I stand at the door and knock. If anyone hears my voice and opens the door, I will come in and eat with him, and he with me.
   (Revelation 3:20)

CLOSING QUESTIONS

1. Are you a sinner?
2. Do you want forgiveness for your sins?
3. Do you believe Jesus died on the cross for you and rose again?
4. Are you ready to invite Jesus into your heart and into your life?

After asking question #4, be silent and pray. Don't say anything more. Your silence is a positive encouragement to them. If they respond in the affirmative, then it's time for them to pray for the forgiveness of their sins, and for the Lord Jesus to become their Savior.

PRAYER

Encourage them to verbalize their prayer in their own words. However, if they are uncomfortable doing this, here is a sample prayer they can repeat after you...

Dear Lord Jesus, I know I am a sinner and I deserve to pay my own sin debt, but I do believe that you died for me to pay the debt that I owe. Today, the best I know how, I trust you as my Savior. I will depend on you from this moment on for my salvation. Now help me to live for you and to do my best to be a good Christian. Thank you Lord Jesus, Amen.

Remember, it's not about you, and what you may or may not say, but what the Word of God has to say. Never ever forget that!

Obviously, what you've just quickly read is a simple outline not including typical responses to the questions. But, you'll be surprised at how compelling and informative these questions are. Again the main thrust is to not allow the conversation to expand into a long, drawn out conversation about you or anything else including... God forbid... an argument. No, God wants us to be the delivery agent in placing the actual Word of God in front of people, and allowing the Spirit of God to do the drawing and convincing through the words of His Bible.

Listen to what Paul has to say to the Thessalonians about this.

For we know, brothers loved by God, that he has chosen you, because our gospel came to you not simply with words, but also with power, with the Holy Spirit and with deep conviction. You know how we lived among you for your sake.
(1 Thessalonians 1:4–5)

Do you want to experience REAL spiritual power? The truth is, whenever the Bible is presented, heard and obeyed, lives are changed! Not just with words as indicated above, but with the Holy Spirit entering into the heart of the individual. The Bible is not only a historical document; it is the "Power of God" to everyone who believes.

Then, from the human perspective, you may say something like this. *"I'm just not cut out to aggressively attempt to walk somebody through the plan of salvation. You may call it fear, or whatever, but I believe God wants me to be a witness simply by how I live my life."*

My friend, this is your choice and far be it for me to dictate how you should live your life before God. Regardless, the Scriptures are clear about the expectations God has planned for us to abide by.

It is true that the Lord has given each one of us different gifts. Gifts that will allow us to serve Him in the best possible way according to the talents and inclinations, we received at birth. That being true, we should never limit how those talents may be used. There are literally hundreds of people who have come to experience the joy of winning another person to Christ. That joy found its resting place in their lives simply because they allowed God to do whatever He wanted to do, by having an open mind to His nudging and leading.

The following Scripture will conclude our study of "Key Imperative" #5.

Therefore, I urge you, brothers, in view of God's mercy, to offer your bodies as living sacrifices, holy and pleasing to God—this is your spiritual act of worship. Do not conform any longer to the pattern of this world, but be transformed by the renewing of your mind. Then you will be able to test and approve what God's will is—his good, pleasing and perfect will. For by the grace given me I say to every one of you: Do not think of yourself more highly than you ought, but rather think of yourself with sober judgment, in accordance with the measure of faith God has given you. Just as each of us has one body with many members, and these members do not all have the same function, so in Christ we who are many form one body, and each member belongs to all the others. We have different gifts, according to the grace given us. If a man's gift is prophesying, let him use it in proportion to his faith. If it is serving, let him serve; if it is teaching, let him teach; if it is encouraging, let him encourage; if it is contributing to the needs of others, let him give generously; if it is leadership, let him govern diligently; if it is showing mercy, let him do it cheerfully. (Romans 12:1–8)

CHAPTER 6

MSM – Key Imperative #6

A Move to Godly Action on His Promptings

The first 5 Imperatives in Action

[*Taking positive action in total compliance with promptings provided by the Holy Spirit of God. Action driven by belief, obedience, a seeking heart, faith and a fearless ability to speak out for the life purpose God has provided.*]

Everything you've read so far has certainly directed your thoughts towards the many scriptural admonitions about serving God, about listening to the promptings of God, and about understanding His will for your lives. Now, I'd like to shift gears and give you a few real-life stories which will give meaning and purpose to what you've learned.

The first one is a recent e-mail from Toni our oldest daughter, who lives in Fayetteville Georgia, a suburb of Atlanta. This e-mail is one of those, "keeping you up-to-date" kind of things.

For you to make good sense of this e-mail, I need to preface the story with this information... Bruce and Toni have been in the ministry for a number of years, and have recently set out to share with the world what God has done in their lives concerning a very specific approach in the teaching of "Forgiveness," something God has called them to share with individuals and churches anywhere he decides to lead them. The following actual e-mail from Toni is just a simple example of how God expects all of his children to act on His "Inspired Direction" for their lives. Listen up!

Hey Mom!

We had ANOTHER incredible day yesterday!

At the Bible study group I was leading, when a woman who has been coming for a year and has been argumentative on occasion – saying things like "It is NOT about God, it's about ME!" – Finally bowed her knees in tears and received Christ! This happened when another woman in the group asked to wash her feet because she heard God tell her to *(like most of us, she had never done this before)* and in the process of having her feet washed, she accepted Christ after we prayed over her. Amazing! *(She has many, many health issues in her life right now as well as family difficulties.)* Praise God!!! *Also...*

Bruce, after teaching his class yesterday morning, was on his way to teach on forgiveness, *"Forgiveness in a Capsule"* at a prominent ministry in Atlanta. One of his students heard he was going and said, I know the leaders of this ministry and they are struggling in their marriage. After Bruce completed his teaching he went to seek out the leaders. Long story short – he spent (4) hours with both the wife and her husband separately. They were scheduled to meet with a judge TODAY to finalize their divorce. Well, they are not getting divorced now! She was rejoicing at the end.

On his way home, late, he didn't realize that he had laid his Bible on the back of the car. Another car came up behind him and began honking just before he was about to get on the Interstate. He pulled over. This couple, from Africa, said, *"It looks like there is a Bible on the back of your car."* Bruce was so grateful for the alert. This Bible was his father's ... very special. Bruce told them where he had just come from and how God used him to save a marriage, then they said, "We are in the ministry too. We pastor a church and are on our way *right now* to meet with a couple who are headed for divorce!" How ironic! Bruce gave them the VERY quick version of what he teaches. They took our card and said, "We want you to come to our church and teach this subject to our people."

Love you – Toni

Now, you could look at the above story with our standard human skepticism, or, you can view it as the hand of God doing what he does best, *(which is everything)* and that is to guide and direct each one of His children along the path of their life, so that others will be able to enjoy the "Grace of God," as He begins to work in their lives as well.

To you, this is just one example, and could very easily fall in the category of "good luck." If you've already read MSM, you would understand there is no such thing as good luck. Everything that happens to every person that walks this earth is directed by God, either through His "Direct or Permissive Will." Since God knows the end from the beginning, *including the heart attitude of all of His children,* and that His desire is for each and every one of them, to come to the saving knowledge of His Son Jesus Christ. This is God's desire in a nutshell!

You may say, "If this is true, then God knows who will follow Him and who won't" and, you're right in that assumption. But, the kicker is, WE DON'T! [So] knowing God will not force Himself on anyone... when we come to Him in faith believing, He will lead us, just as you saw in the story above.

As someone who has walked with God for literally decades, and has experienced the unmistakable leading and guiding by the hand of God, the desire to see others experience that same joy cannot be trapped inside my heart. It must find expression! That expression is what the "Gospel" is all about, telling the wonderful news of God's grace to others, so that they can experience the same joy and love of God as they begin to experience a new partnership, a partnership with God which will last forever.

Years ago, when our children were very young, Gale and I decided to develop our own personal statement of faith in story form. When we would go on vacation, we could hand it out to strangers we would meet along the way. After one of these vacations, we received a letter from a gas station attendant who could not thank us enough for our story. He went on to explain his own personal situation to some extent, and to tell us of his newfound faith in Jesus! Only God knows, how many others were affected in a similar way?

You get the picture, and if you're already a born-again believer in our Lord, I'm sure you have experienced many similar stories in your life.

There is no purpose in belaboring this point, and the message is clear... God wants us to put feet and voice and a heartfelt desire into action on his behalf, as we all walk through this life He has given us. He expects action... Not just out of duty, but of love for those yet bound and tied, or imprisoned within their own false assumption of what life is all about.

As you read this book, maybe it's about time for you to take inventory of your relationship with God. Are you a born again believer who is on fire for Him, or have you been willing to believe that it's okay to sit on the sidelines and let others do what you should be doing? My friend, it's not okay! There is a coming judgment in Heaven for the Christian. It's called in Scripture, *"The Judgment Seat of Christ."* This is not a judgment for the sins we have committed after coming to know the Lord as our Savior, because all of our sin, past, present and future, was paid for on the cross by Jesus. No, this judgment is all about what we've done for Christ AFTER being born into His kingdom. It's that moment in heavenly time, when we will stand before our Lord and He will reward us for service to Him. As we stand in His presence, my question is; will we be rubbing shoulders with those who are there because of the effort we have made personally on their behalf?

Please let me assure you, this book is not about creating a guilt trip for the reader, but is meant solely for the purpose of encouragement.

Then you will know the truth, and the truth will set you free." (John 8:32)

When we know the truth of God's word, and accept it at face value, there is no room for guilt. We are only guilty before God when we reject His commands. Does that make sense? All of us have to come to the point of realizing our eyes are not always open to the truth of God's word. Either on purpose or out of nothing more than just plain ignorance of what His word has to teach us.

When the light of God's word is turned on within our minds and hearts, we can achieve much for the

Lord and those around us who also need what only He can provide! But, it's up to us to step up to the plate. Every person who chooses salvation, by the Grace of Jesus Christ, is a home run. With one swing of the bat, someone has the opportunity to find Home...God calls it Heaven! Are you in the game, or are you using the bat just to lean on, to support you and you alone?

Once again action...or better yet... the verb...acting or doing, producing, seeking, finding, blessing, loving... were all involved in the life of Jesus. The greatest act He performed was presenting Himself to the Father as the one and only single substitute, and payment for the Sin of the world.

The Father sent Him for this purpose, and He never hesitated in His action. He never looked for a way out. He was about His Father's business, just as He told His mother on one occasion when He was just a boy.

People, you need to realize personally... Jesus Christ, the Messiah came, lived, and died for me! Think of it that way! Just for me! And that "me" is for everyone who has ever walked the face of the earth.

We must not be guilty of "NOT telling the world of this most fantastic truth."

CHAPTER 7

MSM – Key Imperative #7

A Continual Spirit of Prayer

The central Key that UNLOCKS Faith

[*"Having a prayerful heart in tune with the ever present Holy Spirit of God, a spiritual link to both God the father and God the son, Jesus Christ, for the express purpose of acting on their collective commands for our life, even when the purpose of those actions is totally unknown to us."*]

This command is found in *(I Thessalonians 5:17) (KJV)* and is rendered "pray without ceasing." In the *NIV* version of God's Word, it speaks of the need for a continual communication link with God the father every waking moment of our lives, or to simply quote directly; "pray continually."

Too often we relegate this thing of prayer only to "specific needs" that come our way, and we know in our heart of hearts that only God can take care of the problem. This reality is normal and natural we believe, since we have a life to live, work to perform, thinking to

accomplish, and a boatload of planning to ensure success. But, is this the way God wants us to communicate with Him? I think not! Whoa... Wait just a minute!
It's impossible to pray continually, you might say. Well,
consider the following

We think this way because we have forgotten that
God is not out there in some far-off distant place in the
Universe which requires that we have a special e-mail
address or some special cell phone number which we
occasionally use to communicate with Him. Or, in some
cases, people continue to believe that we can ONLY pray
in church while on our knees. You get the picture!

Here's reality; as a child of God we are in "constant
communication" with the Holy Spirit which abides
within our very being. Wherever we go, or whatever we're
doing, He is there with us. He is constantly leading and
guiding and knows what's in our heart. But in spite
of this, He has commanded us to put words to those
needs. To think seriously about what we should be
seeking Him for. Biblical prayer then, is to realize you
are never alone as a child of God. You can speak to Him
continuously when you know He's there! When you're
with a loved one, do you only talk to them when you
want something? Is there anything which compels you
to talk with them at certain times, or in certain places,
or since they are present with you, you speak your heart
to them. The only difference is the reality that you are
'always' in the presence of the Holy Spirit of God! He's
always listening and He loves communicating with you
"continually." Listen to what Jude has to say: *But you,
dear friends, build yourselves up in your most holy faith
and pray in the Holy Spirit. (Jude 20)* This is praying
in the power and strength of the "Holy Spirit" or, to be
totally spiritually correct, praying in the complete power
of God Himself.

Prayer is not an afterthought when all else fails, as
some might believe. It's the first and foremost action

of a compelling force which God commands us to do. It defines our view and actions, in taking our faith and confidence in God, as the first step in the process of changing all of our problems and difficulties, including health, sickness, proper life direction, security, godly use of finances, to name a few... All brought before the Lord. This "first" action provides power of unlimited understanding. It speaks to our Savior, and demonstrates our complete trust in Him.

What follows below, are 25 randomly selected Bible verses where the word <u>pray</u>, <u>prayed</u>, or <u>praying</u> are used as part of the verse subject matter. It is interesting to note that when the entire Bible is searched for the word "pray," there are 365 locations involving the use of this word in these three forms.

Far be it for me to suggest this is true as a suggestion for us to pray 365 days a year. But, at least, it's a unique reality. Hmmm? I'd call that "praying continually," wouldn't you?"

As you read each individual verse you will no doubt be prompted to want a better understanding of the context. So, may I suggest that you stop, take your Bible, and gain a greater appreciation of the importance of prayer, or at least make note and return to this location when more time is available. Doing this will engender additional questions increasing your desire to know more about the Word of God and what it can teach you personally. The similarity of putting salt and pepper on your eggs in the morning is inescapable. The new taste for God's word gets better and better because each encounter breeds new questions requiring new answers, and... It's all there just for the asking!

Remember...there are 340 more! Do your own search and find them! Enjoy...! You're now listening to GOD! Digest each verse... don't be in a rush!

I prayed to the LORD my God and confessed: "O Lord, the great and awesome God, who keeps his covenant of love with all who love him and obey his commands." (Daniel 9:4)

But I tell you: Love your enemies and pray for those who persecute you. (Matthew 5:44)

But when you pray, go into your room, close the door and pray to your Father, who is unseen. Then, your Father, who sees what is done in secret, will reward you. And when you pray, do not keep on babbling like pagans, for they think they will be heard because of their many words. Do not be like them, for your Father knows what you need before you ask him. (Matthew 6:6-8)

Watch and pray so that you will not fall into temptation. The spirit is willing, but the body is weak. (Matthew 26:41)

Bless those who curse you, pray for those who mistreat you. (Luke 6:28)

Then Jesus told his disciples a parable to show them that they should <u>always</u> pray and <u>not give up</u>. (Luke: 18:1) (Added emphasis)

Be always on the watch, and pray that you may be able to escape all that is about to happen, and that you may be able to stand before the "Son of Man." (Luke 21:36)

On reaching the place, he said to them, "Pray that you will not fall into temptation." (Luke 22:40)

After Jesus said this, he looked toward heaven and prayed: (John 17:1)

I pray for them. I am not praying for the world, but for those you have given me, for they are yours. (John 17:9)

"My prayer is not for them alone. I pray also for those who will believe in me through their message, that all of them may be one, Father, just as you are in me and I am in you. May they also be in us so that the world may believe that you have sent me. (John 17:20-21)

They devoted themselves to the apostles' teaching and to the fellowship, to the breaking of bread and to prayer. (Acts 2:42)

While they were stoning him, Stephen prayed, "Lord Jesus, receive my spirit." (Acts 7:59)

In the same way, the Spirit helps us in our weakness. We do not know what we ought to pray for, but the Spirit himself intercedes for us with groans that words cannot express. (Romans 8:26)

Be joyful in hope, patient in affliction, faithful in prayer. (Romans 12:12)

I keep asking that the God of our Lord Jesus Christ, the glorious Father, may give you the Spirit of wisdom and revelation, so that you may know him better. I pray also that the eyes of your heart may be enlightened in order that you may know the hope to which he has called you, the riches of his glorious inheritance in the saints, and his incomparably great power for us who believe.... (Ephesians 1:17-19)

And pray in the Spirit on all occasions with all kinds of prayers and requests. With this in mind, be alert and always keep on praying for all the saints. (Ephesians 6:18)

And this is my prayer: that your love may abound more and more in knowledge and depth of insight. (Philippians 1:9)

And we pray this in order that you may live a life worthy of the Lord and may please him in every way: bearing fruit in every good work, growing in the knowledge of God... (Colossians 1:10)

Devote yourselves to prayer, being watchful and thankful. (Colossians 4:2)

With this in mind, we <u>constantly</u> pray for you, that our God may count you worthy of his calling, and that by his power he may fulfill every good purpose of yours and every act prompted by your faith. (2 Thessalonians 1:11) (Added emphasis)

Is any one of you in trouble? He should pray. Is anyone happy? Let him sing songs of praise. Is any one of you sick? He should call the elders of the church to pray over him and anoint him with oil in the name of the Lord. And the prayer offered in faith will make the sick person well; the Lord will raise him up. If he has sinned, he will be forgiven. Therefore confess your sins to each other and pray for each other so that you may be healed. The prayer of a righteous man is powerful and effective. (James 5:13-16)

Husbands, in the same way be considerate as you live with your wives, and treat them with respect as the weaker partner and as heirs with you of the gracious gift of life, so that nothing will hinder your prayers. (1 Peter 3:7)

But you, dear friends, build yourselves up in your most holy faith and pray in the Holy Spirit. (Jude 1:20)

The smoke of the incense, together with the prayers of the saints, went up before God from the angel's hand. (Revelations 8:4)

As can be seen by these selected Scriptures you've just read, God is teaching us that <u>everything</u> in life is important to Him. If it's important to Him, it should be important to us as well. When we were without Christ in our life, when we thought it was all up to us... our choices, our desires, and our plans for the future, we were living in our own strength and direction. At some point, all of us must come to the conclusion that there is more to life than we'll ever be able to grasp, more to the truth of our spiritual nature, the condition it's in, and how it's affecting how we live each day. When we finally reach this point, it's decision time.

We must choose between God and Satan. To some, there will be disbelief in this biblical concept, but one look at this world, and everyone, without question, should realize the truth of good and evil. When the choice is made to follow God, the conversation begins! A daily, moment by moment, conversation with the God of the Universe who has moved into our hearts and minds and bodies to help us live a victorious, joyful and powerful life, impossible to experience in any other way. *MMSM*

How do we experience this conversation? God simply calls it prayer. An ongoing, lifelong personal relationship that will boggle your mind as you see things begin to happen which wouldn't have happened without His leadership showing you the way. Helping you move mountains, the mountains of pain, difficulty, and heights beyond anything you can imagine you could ever climb on your own. *Also, remember it's a conversation! Listen for His response.*

Love is an attitude; love is a prayer
for someone in sorrow, a heart in despair;
Love is goodwill for the gain of another;
Love suffers long with the fault of a brother.
Anon

Through daily consistent time in prayer, in talking to God, in knowing the presence of His Holy Spirit is guiding and leading you... life now has a purpose far beyond the simple thoughts that all of us entertain as we think of what tomorrow might bring for us. *With the above in mind, here is an all-important concept which you may have never thought about before, which I bring to you in story form.*

Have you ever heard someone say about a specific person; *"You know... George has an unbelievable "presence" about himself!" When he walks into a room everybody takes notice! Why is that true do you think? Well...*

For some reason, George automatically grabs everyone's attention, and in some cases there is a hush that comes over the room. Why is George so special? Why do you think he's so respected, and people wait in anticipation of what he might say? Allow me to provide some food for thought.

George is NOT a product of what has happened in his life, but rather George is a product of what he *"thinks has happened in this life."*

What has happened in each of our lives isn't necessarily the basis of what we think has happened in each of our lives. Do you get my drift?

Okay, here's the deal, each one of us is the owner of a certain "presence." The presence we exhibit before others is totally dependent on who we think we are before God. If we know who we are before God, there may be a significant difference in how we look at ourselves than if we didn't know! *This is not just a "play" on words...*

Let's go back and analyze George for a moment. You'd probably agree with me if I were to say... George seemed self-assured, confident, educated in what he had to say, was a good listener, and in many ways he exhibited a tremendous amount of love for other people. Most people seemed to enjoy being around him. He was most always encircled with people looking for answers, and felt it was worth their time in talking to him.

Allow me to add... don't rush too quickly beyond this attribute of being a good listener. Have you ever encountered the individual who, after hearing a few words escape your mouth, proceeds to butt in and conclude your statement for you while adding something they feel you don't know anything about? He or she may be correct in what they've added, but now you are correctly unhappy with them for not allowing you to conclude your thoughts. This individual is projecting an unloving presence, and most likely is not aware of it. They certainly wouldn't pass the "George" test! If he was "George," he would have waited and replied something like this: "Your right, but did you know...?" That's called conversation, not domination in a one-sided conversation.

As you visualize this scenario, and begin to think about yourself, understand this; George did not allow the negative things of life, or personal pride in himself, or the problems he experienced that were not of his doing, paint a picture that he would live out daily in his life. No, George understood how "God" wanted him to live out his life experience on this planet. He did not allow his experiences to control who he knew he really was. He was not re-actionary, he simply took action, and clearly it was "positive action" in displaying before others what he knew in his heart, God wanted him to do.

He educated himself on what God wanted him to be before others. He spent the necessary time in studying the powerful life giving truths of the Word of God... how he should treat and communicate with others, and how he could be of help to them. He knew he should be devoid of sin as much as he could possibly accomplish in this regard. He knew he couldn't be all things to all people, but he did his best to be as much as he could be before them. He seemed to always have time for everyone. Simply stated, he was simply a "Christian" in the truest sense of the word! Moreover, as believers, our exhibited "presence" should be the reflection of "God's Presence." We declare Him, and not self, when we mirror His unmistakable will in our daily walk. To have "presence" in the eyes of others, and be effective in their lives, is to pray the wonderful words of Thomas O. Chisholm, in the refrain of his song;

"O to be like Thee!"

Oh to be like Thee! Oh to be like Thee, Blessed Redeemer, pure as Thou art! Come in Thy sweetness, come in Thy fullness—
stamp thine own image, deep on my heart.

The following biblical admonition stands out and speaks to the child of God, proclaiming the simplicity of exhibiting the "presence" of God.

Dear friend, do not imitate what is evil but what is good. Anyone who does what is good is from God. Anyone who does what is evil has not seen God.
(3 John 1:11)

George knew he was only able to accomplish Gods desire for his life because of one word, and that word is prayer... His time before God on a continuing basis whether working or studying or relaxing was a time of virtual ongoing consistent prayer, or communion with God. To say it another way, his ability to achieve the Presence of God in his life was not of his doing, but was the reflection of the Holy Spirit in answer to his quest to be like Jesus.

To sum it up, Prayer, plus knowing the Word of God, equals "presence." Godly Presence!

Finally, our time of prayer is a love gift to God. He yearns to hear our voice, to respond in kind, and speak to us because He knows we are listening! Yes, my friend, He does speak to us... not in audible tones, but in unmistakable ways too numerous to attempt to explain. But, with the above in mind, I need to leave you with this understanding... When prayers are "said," it becomes nothing more than a voiceless attempt to fulfill a duty usually required by a man made, man driven body of religion.

Make no mistake God is never compelled by "religion!" God is never duty bound by anything man's mind can conjure up, but is only willing to respond when love for Him is true and obvious. Is love the driving force when you pray, or is it only a dutiful act of following religious dogma? "Saying prayers" which are written and are usually repeated on a regular basis, may be acceptable to the church, but unless it's from a heart of love, personal love, demonstrated by a personal voice from the individual... his or hers own message to God, it's nothing more than a repeated act of duty, over and over... just words, lifeless words! Yet we see this happening over and over again simply because the people are instructed to do so by the church.

Prayer is a major part of our relationship to God. It's the underpinning of a truthful desire to know God, and to seek His leadership and direction for the life He has provided. It's Worship to the core!

With the above in mind, listen to what God's word has to say; "*When I called, they did not listen; so when they called, I would not listen,' says the LORD Almighty."* *(Zechariah 7:13)*

Prayer is a two-way street. We are first admonished to "listen to God." How...? As a Christian, a child of God, we are in the position to hear God speak, and as such, we must take action on His specific promptings. It's like the old TV show line... *"Beam me up, Mr. Spock!"*.

God beams us up spiritually, when we have our ears, heart and mind tuned into His channel. The Israelites effectively turned their collective backs on God, refusing to "listen" to His voice provided by His prophets. Verse 14 tells us of God's action, which until 1948, some 2500 years in the making, scattered the Jews among the nations.

"I scattered them with a whirlwind among all the nations, where they were strangers. The land they left behind them was so desolate that no one traveled through it. This is how they made the pleasant land desolate." *(Zechariah 7:14)*

Nothing has changed! God still is a relentless, righteous judge. Doesn't it then make sense to "listen intently" to Him? If we make sure we listen intently, He will speak, direct, lead, provide answers, love and have compassion for every aspect of our life.

What could be better than that? From the story above, George certainly understood. How about you?

Part 3

The Applied Dynamics of The Christian Life

"Biblical Men and Women" Under the Control and Care of the Master

CHAPTER 8

Challenges We All Face

"Whether a New or Mature Christian"
A veritable potpourri of human experience...
in no special order

As we leave what we have learned about George, it's important to note that there are few people capable of embodying all of those unbelievable, wonderful attributes demonstrated in this fictitious example. Some may, *more than others,* reach a point in life, of exhibiting this kind of positive and godly behavior. I believe we all want to be the best we can as God's children in His world of making a difference. Certainly, the "Life of Christ" is our singular most important pattern to follow. To be called "Christian" is the honor of all honors.

With this in mind... and then also to have the following understanding...

Faith, *in a nutshell* is: "Confident Trust," trust in God's promises, and because of this, a life of obedience, filled with total trust in Him. This is pleasing to our Lord and Savior, Jesus Christ. We're now in a position to accomplish much for Him.

But let me get personal. What does trust mean to you? Have you thought about it very much? We all need to realize the baseline importance of this word trust. The following questions are simple, but are all important questions, which occur on a daily basis, and are answered by each of us without our even thinking about it.

You place your confidence, *again that is,* "confident trust" in all sorts of things... The car you drive, the airplane you board, the pilot who sits at the controls... and on and on we could go. But, when we suggest the simple, but profound act of putting our "trust" in God our maker, the one which loves us beyond explanation, we somehow rebel and turn down His unbelievable offer of salvation, securing our eternal life. All of these different objects of trust aren't necessarily things we can see, in order to believe that they are real, but when it comes to God, since we can't see or hear Him audibly speak to us; His importance means little to us. Here's the reason. When we understand who it is that controls our thought patterns every waking moment of our existence, then rejection of God is not difficult to understand.

This is the reason Jesus, after His resurrection, sent the third person of the Trinity, the "Holy Spirit" to overcome the power of Satan working in the lives of all of God's children. Think of it! As a non-believer in the reality of Jesus Christ, God's Son, and the Holy Spirit, you are under the control of the God of this world... Satan! The Bible, the Word of God, is as clear as a bell regarding the truth of this statement. All we have to do is look around at what's going on in this world to confirm it. That said, the only answer for this dilemma, is God!

For the child of God, there is another truth you need to understand as you begin to interact more with people concerning their relationship with God. Believe it or not, people are "being used" by God regardless of their relationship to Him. When God leads His children, He may use others in the process; others who may have not yet come to salvation through Him. We should understand that God's intentions are to create! To make "new" His will in, and through those He deems as needed to help in the process. So, when God leads us, he does so in this fashion. It must be said; people in general, do not have a clue as to how God is using them to accomplish His plan. This will show up in many ways. Here's an example you can multiply... times two, because it's happened in my life.

Most of us have experienced this un-pleasant occasional need... being forced to stop and fix a flat tire! *UGG!* As Darrell & Darrell might say, *"it ain't no fun, but somebody's gotta do it!"* Just like you, I have been the recipient of this wonderful experience a number of times in my life, but on two particular occasions, no sooner had I pulled off the road, and got out of the car; another car came swooping in behind me. The driver roared out of the front seat, and was on a mission! He quickly brushed me aside, and asked me "Does your spare have air in it?" "It better, I replied!" It wasn't but a few minutes, before he was finished and was ready to leave. I offered to give him something for his time and effort, but he would have none of it! I thanked him, and ask God to bless him. His parting comment was, *"Mr. Park, this is something I just do!"* It was his gift to a fellow human being. Little did he know that I was running late, and being all dressed up, did not need to have this happen, but God knew! And then there was the story in MSM concerning my boss Frank when he decided to take me out of the Toledo job. He later learned that God had used him without his ever knowing it!

And we know that all things <u>work together</u> for good to them that love God, to them who are the called according to his purpose. (Romans 8:28) (KJV) (Added emphasis)

"Work together!" This is God in action, in control, and according to His purposes. This is "connectivity," and is what happens in the life of each of His children. We are what we are, by His design and choice, in order to fulfill His goals. We will never fully understand all of them, but we slowly begin to see unusual situations emerge as each day of our life unfolds. So... we should expect and anticipate marvelous days ahead, knowing He is still using us as a tool in His workshop called Earth.

"The Beginning"

Well, not the first beginning, but the beginning of the church as we know it. *(This is not a definitive historical study, but just a brain-teaser to consider.)*

In reading 3rd John, I couldn't help but stop and muse what it must've been like living in those times as a new believer in the life and purpose of Jesus Christ. This Scripture dramatically caught my attention, and made me think about the church today; what we now know, what we believe and experience which would not be true, if not for the reality of what transpired over 2000 years ago.

Think of it! How would we respond today when there's a knock at the door, a knock which could well result in upsetting our predetermined valued schedule. A knock guaranteeing the certainty of a messed up house... dirty floors, sheets to change, dishes to wash, food to prepare, a schedule of life all run amok; unplanned money spent to say nothing about the overall inconvenience of what that single knock at the door will bring. Our usual reaction would be something like this; *"You'd think they could've called first!"*

Not so during the early development of the church. This occurred time and again in those early days, and the church was built by these early Christians who depended on the hospitality of many men and women who God used in the spread of the gospel. It was through this needed support of God's "called out early missionaries," that the church prospered and grew, never to be brushed into oblivion, but to be the single most important historical and spiritual life changing event of all time, which will never, ever cease to exist! It was God's plan to form the church through human instrumentality, with Jesus Christ at the center of it all! But again, once more, think of it! If not for the hospitality of these early church believers, the church might not be here today.

Now listen to John as he paints the picture of this reality...

The elder... To my dear friend Gaius, whom I love in the truth.

Dear friend, I pray that you may enjoy good health and that all may go well with you, even as your soul is getting along well. It gave me great joy to have some brothers come and tell about your faithfulness to the truth and how you continue to walk in the truth. I have no greater joy than to hear that my children are walking in the truth. Dear friend, you are faithful in what you are doing for the brothers, even though they are strangers to you. They have told the church about your love. You will do well to send them on their way in a manner worthy of God. It was for the sake of the Name that they went out, receiving no help from the pagans. We ought therefore to show hospitality to such men so that we may work together for the truth. (3 John 1: 1-8)

Gaius was just one of many who opened their doors to people like Paul and Silas and John and Peter, just to name a few. The church would not be here today if it weren't for people like him. He was to view these godly strangers as if they were God Himself! There were many like him as the church expanded and spread across the borders of many countries. But let me pause...

I would be remiss if I did not share with you the heart's desire of my wonderful wife Gale. Hospitality is her main suit! Her life gives meaning to the phrase "Open Door Policy." Please allow me to share her heart's desire with you.

There has been no greater joy for her, than to open the doors of our house to friends and strangers alike. She views our home as God's house, not ours. Whatever it takes, whenever it happens, she is there for those-in-need, whatever the case. She has always taken great joy in providing joy to others. Example; every year at Christmas time, for a number of years, she provided a sit-down dinner for a large number of people of all strata's in life, be they poor or rich to come and enjoy, all at the same time; creating the need for people to accept each other just as they are as they sit together at the table. This usually took place in early December, at the time of our Church Choir Christmas program. She would invite specific customers of hers, neighbors, and again, people of all walks of life, as a way to be a witness for Jesus Christ. And let me emphasize, this was not a hotdog meal, this was the real thing; a first-class effort, not to impress, but simply to be a witness of the shared grace of God in our lives.

When visiting singers would come to our church, she immediately made sure that she had the opportunity to have them over to the house after church. You'll recall, if you've read MSM, about Park Place, where it was her joy to be used of God in the lives of many, many young people. She was just another Gaius, but God spelled her name Gale!

(You can read more in MSM, chapter 11, entitled... "The love of my life")

In conclusion, there are thousands, if not millions, of churches all over this globe called Earth, which are in existence because of dedicated people like Gaius. Talk about simplicity in marketing? God, in His omniscience, knew long beforehand what the result would be of this approach in the development of His church. One more time... Think of it! The simplicity of the tool of hospitality, working in the hearts and lives of God's people, has brought about the development of God's church and His wonderful plan of salvation to all who would believe.

"Peering Deeply"

Be wise in the way you act toward outsiders; make the most of every opportunity. Let your conversation be always full of grace, seasoned with salt, so that you may know how to answer everyone. (Colossians 4:5-6)

You'll agree I believe, people are constantly checking each other out! It's a "human thing" to accept or reject people we meet. The child of God is expected by God, to accept EVERYONE, irrespective of any and all foibles they may have been born with! This being true, God gives us the grace to *"peer deeply"* into the hearts and minds of everyone we come in contact with. We are able to do this without injury to the new acquaintance. How? By showing unrestricted love and unlimited compassion, while expecting nothing in return. The result is stunning, to say the least! Maybe you've been the recipient of this kind of love, even from a total stranger. You were delighted, and so was God. When filled with MSM, the sky's the limit when it comes to life changing action.

Are there strangers in your life? No one is a stranger to Jesus! Therefore, they should not be to the child of God, even to, and including the hardened criminal...

the individual who would "steal you blind" if given the chance, or maybe even something more frightening! Regardless, our vision of them should be a 300 dpi picture of their never dying soul in an eternity apart from God. Is God able to "save" anyone regardless of their sin and guilt which has caused inexplicable pain and hurt, to many people? Or, is He only interested in those who are generally, so-called "good" people...? You know the answer, don't you? What a glorious privilege it is, to know God provides the ability to "peer deeply!"

"Worldly Worries"

Still others, like seed sown among thorns, hear the word; but the worries of this life, the deceitfulness of wealth and the desires for other things come in and choke the word, making it unfruitful. (Mark 4:18-19) (Added emphasis)

Looking for money? Know this; wealth, status and power mean nothing to God! Is money our only reason for living? What you have in your heart is what matters to God, not what is in your purse, wallet or Bank Account...! Similarly, there's this question... are there "negative" actions we are guilty of taking in life? This may seem like an irrelevant question... Who's not guilty? Sin snowballs in our life most often, if we desire to follow what tempts us. Know this truth... God is never guilty of tempting us in any way. His direction for our lives, is in keeping with His godly perspective, a perspective driven by His love and purpose, aiming at heavenly goals in bringing people to the Savior... not building a Bank Account. God "tests" but does not tempt! Temptation is; "luring over us," and God never does that, but he allows it to happen through the working of Satan in our lives, in order to build our character. When we are true to God, we "see" Satan's temptation for what it is, providing us with a greater understanding of good and evil.

There is a stunning difference in God's value system and the world's, which is based on MPP; Money, Power and Pleasure. Contrary to these, are Joy, Provision and Strength which only comes... how? It comes by securing a new and personal relationship with God, through His salvation process. This then results in His gift, of our personal measure of Faith. *(MSM)*

For this reason I remind you to fan into flame the gift of God, which is in you through the laying on of my hands. For the Spirit God gave us does not make us timid, <u>but gives us power, love and self-discipline</u>. So do not be ashamed of the testimony about our Lord or of me, His prisoner. Rather, join with me in suffering for the gospel, by the power of God. He has saved us and called us to a holy life—not because of anything we have done but because of His own purpose and grace. This grace was given us in Christ Jesus before the beginning of time, but it has now been revealed through the appearing of our Savior, Christ Jesus, who has destroyed death and has brought life and immortality to light through the gospel. (2 Timothy 1:6-10) (Added emphasis)

"Truthfulness"—A must discipline for the believer! *(More on this later)* It is one requirement which flies in the face of our inbred penchant for deceit (sin). Here we see the Apostle Paul making an appeal to all believers in Jesus Christ, to follow his lead in being a witness for Jesus. God will not bless us, when we hide the truth! To hide truth is to allow those who do not know it, to be deceived continually. This effectively promotes "untruth over truth" and when it comes to money, spoken of above, we find that "Greed stifles Truth." Why? Because, if we tell the truth, we just might be found guilty and therefore suffer loss. We've all seen these kinds of situations where it's better to "keep it to myself, than to tell the truth and be blamed for the problem!" Usually, this is the result of a wrong motivation... it's called Greed!

Then He said to them, "Beware, and <u>be on your guard against every form of greed</u>; for not even when one has an abundance does his life consist of his possessions." (Luke 12:15) (NASB) (Added emphasis)

Have you ever wondered what it would be like to head up a group of people who were on the threshold of finding hidden treasure? Can you imagine how exciting an opportunity this must be? We see stories like this about people who've been made wealthy beyond imagination. As an example, the discoverer's of the Titanic and other treasures. There seems to be a longing in every soul for wealth, whether we're willing to admit it or not. This kind of desire includes fame and popularity as well.

By now, as you've been reading this book, you may realize there is "hidden treasure" of a magnitude impossible to comprehend. The key to the discovery of this buried treasure has been available to all without cost. No investment in large vessels, sonar equipment, and a payroll required for your team, to say nothing about the lurking potential for failure, and even the potential loss of life. Think of the pain of searching and searching, the sweat and never-ending heat of the day, all for what? Just to be rich? To be held in esteem, as one who was willing to gamble everything in search of fame and fortune. And then... You hit pay dirt, you been fortunate enough to discover the hidden treasure.

Now you're rich! Obviously, your excitement is over the top. Question; are you thankful or prideful? Friends, there is only one answer when WE accomplish it, we are full of pride. But, on the other hand, when treasure comes our way through the current of love, we can be nothing but thankful. Do you see the folly of one, and the joy of the other? Which one is temporal, and which one is eternal? Which one do you lose at death, and which one is waiting for you after death? *Grasp the truth of the following scripture...*

Do not be afraid when a man becomes rich, When the glory of his house is increased; For <u>when he dies he will carry nothing away</u>; His glory will not descend after him. Though while he lives he congratulates himself, and though men praise you when you do well for yourself, he shall go to the generation of his father's; <u>they will never see the light</u>. Man in his pomp, yet without understanding, is like the beasts that perish. (Psalm49:16-20) (NASB) (Added emphasis)

Even long before the earthly existence of Jesus Christ, our Redeemer, the writer of this Psalm knew the answer. The "hidden treasure" of God was awaiting Him when He would enter the realm of God. God has clearly pointed all men from the very beginning, to the treasure they should invest their time in seeking. This treasure is God! Throughout time immemorial, the treasure map has been available to all who seek it. Which treasure is more important to you?

"Falsehood"

When you pause and think about it, lying or creating a falsehood is the first rung of the ladder which leads to a multiplication of additional sin. Each and every lie is part of this multiplication process involving, not only the person telling the lie, but many others which are caught in the web of this deceitful action. There are absolutely no redeeming factors involved with telling lies. The idea of there being "white lies," or small and insignificant untruths, is in itself a lie! Some people enjoy telling lies just to see if they can get away with it. They may be successful momentarily, but in the end, it always comes back and bites them!

With these simple truths in mind, it is impossible to have a day-to-day walk with God if you are a lie teller. Do Christians tell lies? Yes they do. If I didn't admit to this truth, I'd be telling a lie. This truth sounds like a dichotomy, but it serves to point out the reality of the presence of sin in all of our lives, whether or not, we have named the name of Jesus Christ as our Savior. We are all still sinners! *Now that's the truth!* To believe otherwise would be a lie. So, how can we walk with God on a day-to-day basis and have a continuing time of fellowship with him?

There's a song which talks about an action we all must be part of if we are to walk with God. It talks about "guarding your heart." It speaks of the need to have your antenna up all of the time when circumstances provide the opportunity to be either truthful or untruthful in order to accomplish a desired goal. We must be willing to recognize this as a teaching moment from God! How can we expect God to bless us when we find ourselves telling lies? This is where, "the end does not justify the means." The other thing; many have told lies for so long in their life, it has become a lifelong habit. Habits are hard to change, but when a person accepts Jesus Christ into their life, they gain a new perspective on what's right and what's wrong. It doesn't take long for them to see how disruptive their life has been because of their lies. There is no magic bullet we can use to shoot the habit of lying out of the sky! But I can guarantee you this, any time you're caught in a lie, or have not yet been caught in a lie, you will know what you've done was wrong before God. If you're reading this, and thinking about your own personal life, and there seems to be no conscious concern about lying, then, my friend, you need to take inventory of your relationship with God. The simple sin of lying can be used as a measuring rod for our relationship with our Lord.

Listen to what the New Testament book of *Ephesians* has to say about God's view of the subject of telling lies, and also the subject of anger.

So I tell you this, and insist on it in the Lord, that you must no longer live as the Gentiles do, in the futility of their thinking. They are darkened in their understanding and separated from the life of God because of the ignorance that is in them due to the hardening of their hearts. Having lost all sensitivity, they have given themselves over to sensuality so as to indulge in every kind of impurity, with a continual lust for more.

You, however, did not come to know Christ that way. Surely you heard of him and were taught in him in accordance with the truth that is in Jesus. You were taught, with regard to your former way of life, to put off your old self, which is being corrupted by its deceitful desires; to be made new in the attitude of your minds; and to put on the new self, created to be like God in true righteousness and holiness.

Therefore <u>each of you must put off falsehood and speak truthfully to his neighbor,</u> for we are all members of one body. "In your anger do not sin:" Do not let the sun go down while you are still angry, and do not give the devil a foothold.
(Ephesians 4:17-27) (Added emphasis)

I included the verse on anger, because anger is usually tied in some way to a falsehood. The apostle Paul could not be any clearer on what you have just read concerning this grievous sin we all have participated in. Oftentimes the lies we tell, and the anger we show, is the result of trying to cover up a previous falsehood. Some feel justified in telling lies in order to maintain their own personal political stance in life. We see this daily when watching television as politicians argue back and forth about their own ideological position on any given subject. In their minds, it's all about winning the argument, not telling the truth. Even when they know, *beyond a shadow of doubt,* that the person they're competing with is correct in their analysis of the subject, they will then conjure up some false pretense or blatant lie to maintain their political position!

Well, the examples are endless, but when you find someone who will not bow down to this sinful action, but will succeed or not succeed when telling the truth of the matter; this person is pleasing to God, and in the ultimate, is the true winner. It would be nice to know the ratio of liars to truth tellers... but only God knows... and that's Okay!

Those which argue about telling little white lies in order to maintain relationships with people, such as when the simple question is asked; "How are you feeling today...?" And the person answers, "I'm feeling great!" When, in reality they just told a lie. So the question is; are these kinds of lies okay with God? Nope! As mentioned earlier, God cannot look upon sin. This being true, what then should the answer be to the above question if a person is in fact, not feeling well, or things are going badly for them? First of all, if we think relationships are held together by a series of untruths, then we do not have a viable relationship at all! This is true because we usually will learn, "the truth of the matter." When truthful discovery is made, relationship confidence is lost!

Back to the honest answer...If you're not feeling great... just say, God's in control, or, I'm fine... but I'm waiting on some answers. If you're not great, don't lie because God is listening to what we say out loud, and also what we say to ourselves. Remember, He's our partner! He's living our lives with us! What could be better?

Summation: do not try to control situations in your life by lying to others about anything! You are literally digging a grave for your personhood. Confidence in you is lost, future believability in anything you say is at risk. Know this; lying is a real big deal! It's a big deal with God, since, if you insist on lying to others, how can you expect God to believe in you when you come to him when in need? Nuff said!

"Will it be Pride... or Gratefulness?"

The heart is deceitful above all things and beyond cure. Who can understand it? (Jeremiah 17:9)

Prestige, power, wealth and even honor, add nothing to our value in the eyes of God. In reality, we are nothing more than a "puff of air," if we limit ourselves just to these goals in life. But, in retrospect, the faithful effort we accomplish for God has eternal consequences. So much of our time is spent in competition with others for all of the above. We seek to climb the ladder of worldly success knowing full well, when the mountaintop has been reached, it's all downhill from there! But, we say that's okay, we'll just do it again.

What does the mountaintop represent... pride? Is there such a thing as "healthy pride" you may ask? Is seeking accomplishment in this life a wrong ambition?

Allow me to answer these questions in this manner. Simply stated; "yes and no," but, only when it is driven by Godly purpose. This whole concept of MSM is all about leading a successful, fulfilling life in compliance with the teachings of Jesus. Our success will not come in our own power, but by the power of God. Aren't you filled with joy, when someone reaches for the stars and is successful, but attributes his or hers success to God, to Jesus Christ, knowing that only with His approval and direction, all accomplishment, apart from Him, is "self-centered" and full of personal pride? This kind of accomplishment is typically short-lived because it is flawed! Its purpose is not eternal, but temporal. Be constantly aware of "creeping pride!" Even in serving God, pride is an insidious, ever 'creeping forward' sin. We most often do not see it coming, much less knowing it's even present now! When present, we find ourselves looking for, and even manufacturing proofs that no pride is present. Not only are we "prideful," but we end up lying about its existence in us! When we're so full of pride, we attempt to take joy internally, by how we are able to explain away our pride with forced actions to prove our so called humility.

Yuck, yuck! We are as guilty as the worst sinner who has ever set foot on the earth! In fact we are the worst sinner! All sin is "sin!" Whether large OR small!

We need to constantly keep our antenna up, sensing the signal of "creeping pride!" But, through God's grace we can show praise to God 'through' those who have excelled in one way or another. When a child of God has made it to the top, and received praise for their accomplishment, they know in their heart of hearts... the glory belongs to God. It's when we stand in awe of how God shows up in our lives, and uses us as a conduit of His love, then pride is replaced by gratefulness and heaven sent joy! This is MSM to the Max! This is why we are alive! *But, every reader needs to understand this...*

This book is an "onslaught" on sin, not the sinner... We are all sinners and it's through the pathway of faith we navigate this life. When we revisit our lives, as I was forced to do in writing MSM, and regardless of age, we begin to recognize the many perils God has smothered and moved out of our pathway. It must be said; we are "saved" daily from the "might have been," to the "painless pathway of peace and joy!" Much sin has perished right before our lives! Things our sinful flesh might desire, but which had been dissolved or crushed before they could infect our very soul. This, my friend, is the purpose and plan of God for building us up for service... How? It's by the power of the ever present Holy Spirit. You may also ask... what role do I play in this ongoing, life preservation scheme of things?

Apart from living for God; not self, it's impossible to empirically develop some sort of "action plan" to help God make everything smooth as silk. *People... it aint' gonna happen!* But, this we do know without a doubt... God's love for the believer shows up in uncanny ways! We are clueless how these things come to be... they just do! They include both good and also unfortunate happenings through the direct or permissive will of God.

The unfortunate has purpose and requires a patient love for God while waiting on the revelation of His purpose. Notice I said, "Patient love for God!" Here's the thing we must all remember... God has no desire to hurt or punish His children unless we deserve punishment. If we carry around an unforgiving attitude, or total un-forgiveness for someone, even when we know God has forgiven us, we should expect a teaching moment ahead! It might well be something not too pleasant! His book is filled with answers. It's up to us to discover them, thus the reason for the writing of this book. All the answers are not here, but you know where they are! Got a problem? Take it to God, or to your Pastor, or someone you know who will enjoy helping you over the hump.

Never Fear, God is here!

"Assumptions"

In order to explain away certain happenings, or certain results, we are prone to making unfounded assumptions, based on partial knowledge or even a deep seated desire for revenge or payback for our experience of pain, grief, or even fear for the future. This can also lead to unwarranted actions, which we may regret in the future, thus multiplying the negative. This must be avoided at all costs, and there is a way out... God's way out! Follow with me as we tackle this subject based on Biblical principles.

Assume God will help.

Abraham replied, "I said to myself, 'There is surely no fear of God in this place, and they will kill me because of my wife.' Besides, she really is my sister, the daughter of my father though not of my mother; and she became my wife. And when God had me wander from my father's household, I said to her, 'this is how you can show your love to me: Everywhere we go, say of me, "He is my brother."
(Genesis 20:11:13)

Abraham failed... he assumed the King, Abimelech was a wicked man, so, like us, he was prone to make a hasty decision to tell a half truth. He thought deceiving the King was the answer to his problem, rather than trusting God. Not only was his decision misguided, but he lied and forced his wife to lie as well, compounding the problem. Had he sought God in the matter, it could have been avoided, and should have been avoided. Wrong assumptions breed results which may affect an entire lifetime! Our jails are full of wrong assumptions. There is a better way!

Assume the best in others. (Numbers 32)

Here we find Moses assuming the three tribes of Israel, Ruben, Gad and the half tribe of Manasseh, which wanted to stay on the east side of the Jordan, rather than cross over into the promised land, were wanting to avoid doing their duty in providing protection to the rest of Israel. They made it clear to Moses; they <u>would not neglect their duty as he had assumed</u>. He relented and things went as originally planned.

How often are WE guilty in jumping the gun, and taking action that is totally uncalled for? Or, even worse, do we find ourselves rehearsing in our minds circumstances about a given situation which we may think is not in our favor, and creating a false picture of what the truth is really all about. It's one thing to think these kinds of thoughts and it's another to take action without first knowing what the real truth is. When this happens, we are guilty of judging another person pre-maturely, even if it's only in our mind and not yet made public. Judging another person falsely, whether it's in our mind, or openly to their face, is still sin.

What's the answer to this kind of thinking? It's all wrapped up in whether or not we tend to look at things positively or negatively. Ultimately, when we're faced with these kinds of situations, it's best to take it to the Lord in prayer asking for His direction and leadership on what we should do next. Our concern should be about seeking truth, and in that seeking, to not allow Satan to take over leadership in our lives. Things usually are not as bad as we may think!

In wrapping up this subject, "Assumptions;" loving each other, regardless of misgivings, personality traits which may be foreign to us, or views some hold which we may be in disagreement with... should always be the attitude of heart we maintain. We should not allow anything to become a wall, or a barrier to our love for one another. Having a heart of love, will also keep us from judging one another based on our own flawed ideas. Real love is an action, not just a feeling!

Assume the best... Not the worst!

"Total Dependence"

While providing a birds-eye view of this subject in the Introduction to the book, some of what you have already read, has provided a few clues to this reality of life. When we think of "total dependence," and not having experienced the in-depth meaning of this term, we may find ourselves thinking, or picturing people like; Missionaries, full-time church workers, and finally, even church Pastors. This thinking process is not uncommon, because we know, from their personal financial point of view; their dependence is on others who give to the church, or the missionary organization they are connected with. Also, we may think this way because there is not a specific product or physical service involved. Therefore, what they do is not unlike that which we pay for when we attend a College or University. It is simply providing an education to those which are interested in seeking that education. But, it must be said, since we pay for this education, we do not view the college professor in the same way we view a paid Sunday school teacher, or church Pastor. We look on the teaching more as a gift from God, not something we pay for. Our financial gifts to God through the church are all encompassing, and relate to all of the church needs, not just the salaries of full time employees of the church.

Historically, and sadly I might add, some have attached ownership over those which spend their life teaching and helping their church members to fully understand the Word of God. It's the mindset which states, "even though you are our pastor or teacher, you are responsible to the Elders of the church in all matters." This mindset has revealed itself in certain "Elder driven church governments." It oftentimes ties the hands of the pastor or teacher in terms of his rightful responsibility as being the biblical leader of the church or class he or she teaches. Those involved as part of the Elder board, which in many cases, enjoy a lifetime appointment, often view their responsibility in the same sense as a business, and taking on a position of power. In this type of governmental approach, the pastor, or teacher is nothing more than an employee of the church.

This kind of church government is at least... a total contradiction of the meaning of faith, and at worst... totally un-biblical! *(Some may not be in agreement with this suggestion, but, I can only speak from personal experience re; the possibility of the following potential outcome, where Elder rule has been involved in an ungodly way)*

This church governmental structure revolves around power, with the power finding its home within the elder board. Sad to say, there are many horror stories where the people of the church, being effectively on the outside looking in, have no say, or voting opportunity to make a difference in the selection of a Pastor and other key employees of the Church Body. Pastors or teachers have been fired, with no opportunity of sharing their case with the church. They are effectively black-balled without recourse. Many good men and women have faced this reality causing irreparable damage in every part of their lives! Physical, emotional, and of utmost importance, spiritual! When this happens, the church membership, which are considered nothing more than sheep, are left to the reality of never knowing why their leaders have been fired. This action breed's discontent at all levels, unanswered questions, unfounded judgmental scenario's, and degrading the character of those involved while giving reasons for the loss of upset church members.

Well, what does all of this have to do with the subject at hand... "Total Dependence"

Firstly, the church is to be led by the power of God, the Holy Spirit, as dictated by scripture. Considering the Pastor; if he's to be successful in his position as leader of the Body of Believers, must be a man of Faith, a man of the Word, a man who exhibits "Total Dependence" on God, not on some earthly organizational structure which lords over all church decisions based on the personal whim of the group at any point in time. He maintains his leadership position as long as he has proven his worthiness to the congregation, and most of all to God. If not, it's up to the church body, guided by a Board of Deacons, to allow him to continue to lead, or if not, to remove him based only on his inability to scripturally maintain his position as Pastor. Anything short of this Congregational Church governmental design, is un-biblical. When seeking a church to attend, make sure its government is in keeping with the biblical design as stated above.

"Total Dependence" isn't limited to the church alone. It's also the cornerstone of Faith. Faith is not faith if it lacks something to have faith in. Not a play on words, but the truth of our relationship with God! Knowing there is a God, and only one God, the God of all cre-ation, how can we live if we don't understand our abso-lute need to be "totally dependent" on Him... Jehovah... that is, God, Jesus, Holy Spirit! The blessed Trinity, one God, but realized in three distinct forms... the Father, Son, and Holy Spirit.

Allow me to get practical here. Whatever the church government is, including the biblical Congregational form outlined above, if decisions are made irrespec-tive of considering spiritual, godly and prayerful action, then God is displeased and His judgment on the church should be expected.

It's always been amazing to me to see wonderful churches fade into oblivion, caused by ungodly decision making on the part of its leadership. A key part of the failure is usually centered on those seeking power and control. Had there been "total dependence" on God, and not on them, these kinds of difficulties quite possibly could have been avoided.

I bring all of the above to your attention, in not only speaking to the individuals need for total dependence on God, but more importantly, to speak to the reality of what's happened in the church over many years and even centuries. All you have to do is to take a look at Europe and the older part of this country, and see the church buildings which are empty, or being used for some other purpose. Where Christianity has become distasteful and considered irrelevant and old-fashioned, if not totally untrue. Where lust for life and modern-day idols have taken over, demonstrating the truth of Scripture as a sign of the times! Listen to what God's word has to say about the subject.

But mark this: There will be terrible times in the last days. People will be lovers of themselves, lovers of money, boastful, proud, abusive, disobedient to their parents, ungrateful, unholy, without love, unforgiving, slanderous, without self-control, brutal, not lovers of the good, treacherous, rash, conceited, lovers of pleasure rather than lovers of God—having a form of godliness but denying its power. Have nothing to do with them. They are the kind who worm their way into homes and gain control over weak-willed women, who are loaded down with sins and are swayed by all kinds of evil desires, always learning but never able to acknowledge the truth. Just as Jannes and Jambres opposed Moses, so also these men oppose the truth—men of depraved minds, who, as far as the faith is concerned, are rejected. But they will not get very far because, as in the case of those men, their folly will be clear to everyone. (Short break...)

Does this sound familiar? Those of you reading this book, which up until this point have, for whatever reason, not enjoyed the reading of God's word, and now are reading... maybe for the first time, what God has to say about this world in which we live, the time were living in, and what we can expect to see happen. The book of *2nd Timothy* was written by the Apostle Paul, and the remainder of this Scripture speaks about his relationship and purpose in serving God after coming out of a life filled with sin and hate for all Christians. God changed his heart and mind!

Follow along with the remaining verses, and if necessary, re-read this total story in order to have it sink deeply into your heart.

You, however, know all about my teaching, my way of life, my purpose, faith, patience, love, endurance, persecutions, sufferings—what kinds of things happened to me in Antioch, Iconium and Lystra, the persecutions I endured. <u>Yet the Lord rescued me from all of them</u>. In fact, everyone who wants to live a godly life in Christ Jesus will be persecuted, while evil men and impostors will go from bad to worse, deceiving and being deceived. But as for you, continue in what you have learned and have become convinced of, because you know those from whom you learned it, and how from infancy you have known the holy Scriptures, which are able to make you wise for salvation through faith in Christ Jesus. <u>All Scripture is God-breathed and is useful for teaching, rebuking, correcting and training in righteousness</u>. (2 Timothy 3:1-16) (Added emphasis)

Remember the song which Frank Sinatra made popular... *"I did it my way?"* Well, we all want to do it our way... and, for the most part there's nothing wrong with that concept. It's not about the doing it's about the leading which is most important. As a born again child of God, we have committed our life to our maker Jesus Christ. In no way is that an abdication of our personal responsibility for the decisions necessary to assure a good life.

Here's the way it works! When we know God, we first of all seek his blessings on what we do. In the process of seeking His blessing, we are forced to consider all of the actions we take from an entirely different perspective. We have come to understand the need to filter all of our desires, thoughts, principles, and actions we take, through the presence of the Holy Spirit which abides within each born-again believer in Jesus Christ. We do this by talking to Him. This is an ongoing, minute by minute, hour by hour, day by day conversation with Him. It's not a one-sided conversation, believe it or not! We ask and he answers. If the answer is yes, we have peace in our heart about the matter. If the answer is no, then we sense this, as a "prodding for us to check deeper into what we want to do."

It's not unlike the school teacher who requires each class member to develop a project of their own. The project may require a certain time limit for its construction. The rules of the game may be questioned by the student, but how the project should be constructed is totally up to them. From time to time, the teacher will walk by, just to see how things are coming along. You can ask all the questions you want, but the only answer you will receive is a Un-huh, or a Un-uh. *(yes or a no!)* Indeed, you may feel helpless! In dealing with the Holy Spirit, I call it a "Godly Un-huh or a Un-uh." To be sure, you'll know in your heart if it's a Yes or No! *(This truth was made clear to me by Toni, our oldest daughter, some time ago. She had it right!)*

Remember the subject above about "Peering Deeply?" When we peer deeply into another person's life, we do it by showing love and compassion for them. When we peer deeply into the Holy Spirit of God who dwells within, we do it the same way... With love and compassion for Him!

To love is to trust. To show compassion is to show empathy or care.

God always responds to our love and compassion for Him. Why? Because He knows what's going on in our minds and hearts. [So] to sum up, if what we want to do with our life passes the test of the Holy Spirit, in terms of His purpose for why He has placed us here on this Earth, we will know by all the above reasons I've just explained. For the brand-new, uninitiated Christian, this may sound Hokey Pokey to you, but believe me, it won't take long before you begin to understand this new language just spoken of, not only for our desires, but also a language which includes His promptings and nudges resulting in placing in our minds, thoughts and actions which need to be taken; prayers that need to be prayed, along with a continuing understanding of what God is all about, His purpose and His desire for your life.

"Sounding the Trumpet"

If you've read MSM, you'll probably recall the story I told, when as a sixth grade student I was involved in a 100 yard dash runoff in order to select someone to compete with a speedy eighth-grader who had recently moved from South America to our area. Well, after competing and beating this new outstanding runner, I was looking forward to high school when I could be part of the track team. After reaching high school, I suffered an injury to my right heel while running track, which forced me off of the track team for good. I was devastated, but dad assured me that God had a reason for this happening, and told me to begin looking at other things I could do well in school. Now, as I look back on this situation, I believe God took me out of the running business, because I could have been overcome with personal pride in my running ability. There is no doubt... my ability to run fast was exceptional, and there is no telling how far up the ladder of success I could have reached, but God knew best!

Since I was always a music buff, I decided on learning how to play the trumpet. Long story short... I was now a trumpeter in the high school band, and occasionally was asked by the local sheriff's department to play taps at the funeral of local soldiers returning from the Korean War. Well, I've been a trumpeter ever since, not in playing the horn, but doing my best to "Trumpet the call of God in everyone's life." That's what these two books are all about.

From the biblical perspective, Ezekiel speaks clearly about "Sounding the Trumpet."

The word of the LORD came to me: "Son of man, speak to your countrymen and say to them: 'When I bring the sword against a land, and the people of the land choose one of their men and make him their watchman, and he sees the sword coming against the land and <u>blows the trumpet to warn the people</u>, then if anyone <u>hears the trumpet but does not take warning</u> and the sword comes and takes his life, <u>his blood will be on his own head</u>. Since he heard the sound of the trumpet but did not take warning, his blood will be on his own head. <u>If he had taken warning, he would have saved himself</u>. But if the watchman sees the sword coming and <u>does not blow the trumpet</u> to warn the people and the sword comes and *takes the life of one of them, that man will be taken away because of his sin, <u>but I will hold the watchman accountable for his blood</u>.' (Ezekiel 6:1-6) (Added emphasis)*

God makes it abundantly clear that both the trumpeter and those that hear the trumpet are both equally accountable to God. There are many ways the child of God can play the trumpet. This truth speaks to the lifestyle of the born-again believer in God. As one of His children, we all are responsible to do our part in seeking to fulfill God's command... *He said to them, "Go into all the world and preach the good news to all creation. (Mark 16:15)*

This lifestyle must include our willingness to share the Word of God in whatever way He has commanded us to. When we do, those who reject the message are no longer our responsibility. But, to be perfectly clear, we should never quit telling them! It's God who determines their ultimate fate! [So] "Grab your Trumpet, and let'er blow!" As a sidelight, this doesn't mean you should "Toot your own Horn!"

Got it?

"Where does the Church fit in?"

Consider God's choice

I've decided to carry this same message from MSM, into this sequel, because it is such an important truth for all to read who love the Word of God. It's simply "<u>Sounding the Trumpet</u>" for all to hear and understand, because of God's plan in instituting the church as His new way to communicate to the world. This is an important question, because, believe it or not, some in Christendom have sought to gain power and prestige over the common man, instead of following the simple, yet profound dictates of Holy Scripture. God's heart is saddened when people allow their sinful nature to rear its ugly head from time to time by taking control when they should be listening for direction from their Savior.

First and foremost, Jesus came to wipe the slate clean of all religiosity and man-made attempts to clean our souls from sin by our own works! The Pharisee of His day was a good example of man-made religious practices attempting to please God by instituting religious rules superseding the Holy Scripture. Anything short of God's biblical plan should be understood for what it is. The question we all need to answer; what's it going to be for me? A man-made church, or a God honored and God directed church?

What follows, is an effort to shine biblical light on the difference between the two and some obvious, and not so obvious church failures in our world today.

Before proceeding further, there's a certain thought pattern we as Christians should entertain, if we are to be pleasing to God. In this regard, have you ever asked yourself this question...? How can I be an encouragement to others in their understanding and practice of the word of God? This question is not meant for pastors and teachers in the church only, but applies to each and every one of us as believers in Jesus Christ. The following Scripture makes this very clear...

Do your best to present yourself to God as one approved, a worker who does not need to be ashamed and who correctly handles the word of truth (2 Timothy 2: 15)

We are commanded to prepare ourselves in being ready to help others as they move forward in their walk with God, as well as to make sure of our own acceptable and correct understanding of Scripture. When we gather together in a Bible study, or when asked a certain question, we should do our best to be helpful to all in developing and growing in their understanding of God's Word as well as being available to teach in the church.

This was one of the very first questions I asked myself, when contemplating the writing of this book. Equally important was not to stand in judgment of another individual, but to express a heart of love and compassion for all. While in the process of doing my best to encourage others, and to help them come to grips with the potential for sin in their lives, I quickly learned I had to be true to the message of scripture over an entire adult lifetime in studying God's message. Then, and only then, in a limited fashion, might I find myself in a position to point out error were it has negatively affected the church, and to be helpful in the lives of others in understanding the truth of scripture.

May what is read here not cause pain or hurt in the heart of any individual, or a reaction of anger or displeasure. Rather, may these words be understood for what they are meant to be; words of concern and love for all who have been victimized by non-biblical teaching and outright deceit and words of correction and love for all who share the responsibility of naming sin and proclaiming the scriptures.

Most of all, may God be exalted and praised as you consider your personal reaction to this message of truth. God, in His teaching of truth, expects from His children a willingness to listen with an open heart and mind, and to change where change is needed. When people of God stand in judgment of other believers, God is not pleased! On the contrary, when people of God are motivated to learn and teach His truth to all who will listen, then God is pleased with their heart of service to Him.

This book is written solely for this purpose...to please God first, and to help promote a truthful understanding of error in the church, error driven out of ignorance of truth, or out of desire for personal gain and the praise of man. The key for all is God's willingness to forgive.

Forgiveness and judgment by man are not compatible, as with oil and water, but love and truth are. Listen as David exalts the truth of "Forgiveness."

Blessed is the one whose transgressions are forgiven, whose sins are covered. Blessed is the one whose sin the LORD does not count against them and in whose spirit is no deceit. (Psalms 32:1-2)

As a potential child of God, or one who has already named the name of Jesus Christ as Savior, there is, and will always be, sin in the church, because we as believers are still sinners! Sinners saved by grace, but still sinners. All are capable of wrongdoing and possible misguided loyalty to sinful teaching and teachers, teachers whom God will judge in His own timing.

Don't expect to find a perfect church, because as His children, we are not perfect. God, in His Word, the Bible, has demonstrated His undying love, and will forgive us daily as we request and seek it! But when we are found in sin, un-forgiven sin, we will be judged accordingly by Him. Fortunately for all of us, He has provided a roadmap powered by Truth and Love. When anything we do, say or think is not lead by faith, truth and love, it is sin. It is in this spirit, this chapter has been written.

Until Christ returns, *lest we forget*, Satan is still the Prince and the Power of the air, and when he can use his convincing satanic deceit designed to separate one believer from another, he will do so. As you will note below, he has had success in perverting the truth surrounding "God's inspiration of the original scriptures or manuscripts."

This is a very important issue, but some may ask the compelling question, why are you venturing into such a controversial subject as the inspiration of scripture and how it relates to the selection of a Bible to study or use today, or, this thing of Cults and un-biblical, so-called churches? Well, for the very same reason that the Apostle Paul was compelled to call out Peter regarding his seeming need to disassociate himself from eating with the Gentiles because of his fear of those who belonged to the "circumcision crowd."

(See Galatians 2:11-21)

Peter needed to hear this admonition from Paul which more fully grounded him in the simple plan of salvation by grace *alone* without works. Therefore, anything which serves to harm the message of God and negatively affect believers, as well as it's proclamation to the world, must be unveiled by the shining light of God's truth for all to see!

To begin with; before extending this discussion, we need to understand the following. As mentioned above, "real truth" emanates *only* from the scriptures, the Bible. Also, remember this truth. When we speak of scripture, we are actually speaking of Jesus! He alone is the living Word. The Bible we read was inspired by Him because He is God! The book of John, in the first five verses makes this abundantly clear. The key operative word John used, is none other than "was." Think of it as you read this portion of Scripture. Jesus... was-is-and will be forever. He is God! He, in statement of truth, is the singular writer of the Holy Scriptures.

In the beginning <u>was</u> the "Word," and the Word <u>was</u> with God, and the Word <u>was</u> God. He <u>was</u> with God in the beginning. Through him all things were made; without him nothing <u>was</u> made that has been made. In him <u>was</u> life, and that life <u>was</u> the light of all mankind. The light shines in the darkness, and the darkness has not overcome it. (John 1:1-5) (Added emphasis)

Therefore, speaking of your church; it just may not be a biblical church based solely on the scriptures. It may even fall into the realm of cultism. There are very powerful main line cults which refer to their Body as a church, but they may "add to the equation" with a connection to the Bible, but only on par with a second book, or books written by the original leader of the cult. These books, may even take precedence over the Bible in their day to day practice.

In the book of Revelation, John includes a final admonition to restrain from adding to the words of scripture, in particular the book of Revelation, and this verse also, strongly implies to the totality of the Canon of Scripture, the Bible. Therefore, those who would have us believe there is something *in addition* to Sacred Scripture, which is necessary for us to know God, and which also promotes another historical figure on a par with the Son of God... will ultimately stand in judgment by God for their actions.

I warn everyone who hears the words of the prophecy of this book: If anyone adds anything to them, God will add to him the plagues described in this book. And if anyone takes words away from this book of prophecy, God will take away from him his share in the tree of life and in the holy city, which are described in this book. (Revelation 22:18-19)

Interestingly enough... just two verses from the end of the Bible!

Let me repeat...these man-driven cults, are in danger of the judgment of God. Also, some of these groups are characterized by intense secrecy and power over the congregation, usually by a ruling council. Excommunication is part of the power invoked, if and when people may speak their honest feelings in disagreement to anything not supported by church dogma. They are literally kicked out of the church and ostracized to the point of possibly losing their jobs! This reality cannot be over emphasized. Everyone at some point needs to honestly take inventory of their spiritual connections; are they God driven or Man driven? These cults are alive and well today! Of course, they do not call themselves a cult, but as you would guess, they refer to themselves as a church.

Now, as I speak to you as possibly a newborn child of God... before you enter into any long-term relationship with any church, be sure to do your homework and due diligence on what this group you're considering, is all about. Have them provide you with their statement of faith, and seek to determine by asking questions whether or not they pass the test of being a true church of God.

Note: this may be accomplished by an "online" review of the church in question, as a first step. Then, secondly, a personal face to face question asking meeting should occur in order to clarify any and all questions. You will find this process to be a mutual method of clarification of belief and teaching for both the church and you personally.

Obviously then the next question is, "what is the true church which God speaks of in His scripture?" [His] church, is the sum total of His earthly family. The only members of His church are those who have become His children by faith in Him and His Gospel; repenting of their sin.

"What then is the true measure of a godly church from the *local perspective?*" Good question! But this is simple too. The local church, where God would have you attend, should have at the center of its worship... Jesus Christ, His method of salvation, which you are reading about here, and a church whose lasting goal is to bring men and women, boys and girls, to the knowledge of Jesus Christ as their Savior; a church where the scriptures are preached and taught to the local congregation; a church which has a world view and vision, supporting the sending out of Missionaries in pursuit of sharing the gospel around the globe; a church whose local government is consistent with the biblical model, and finally, a church which teaches from only one book, the Bible. Also, it is a place where love and compassion for the needs of the people in the local community are demonstrated in an active and regular fashion.

One more time, the Central Command by Jesus Christ Himself was...

He said to them, "Go into all the world and preach the good news to all creation." (Mark 16:15)

This was the very beginning of the spread of the "good news," commonly referred to in the Bible as the gospel, or the evangelization of the entire world. This was, and is true evangelism at its very core, and was the beginning of the founding of the "local" Church Body. The apostle Paul, in his three Missionary journeys was responsible for the founding of many of these early church congregations, and, I might add, they were small in number, so the size of the church is not important. The Bible speaks this truth...

"For where two or three are gathered together in my name, there am I in the midst of them." (Matthew 18:20) (KJV)

As you consider all of the above regarding the church, the most important thing to you personally is your "personal salvation," or relationship with Jesus Christ. Once you've made your commitment to Him, God in His omniscience, *(all knowing)* will lead you to a church which is committed to Him. You can count on it! *MSM*

Second to the above, is the need to completely understand the key to our relationship with our brothers and sisters in Christ, including real love one for another, unbiased love, which might very well be in jeopardy by some forced, unbiblical long held faulty belief by many. As you read the following words I've written here, my purpose is not to leave the impression that I stand in judgment of these my soul mates, but only to voice the words which I have been prompted by the Holy Spirit to write as a way of opening up their hearts and minds... and most importantly, bringing to light the devious power of Satan as he attacks many of God's people without their even being aware of it!

Friends, Satan has found a way to get into our heads! Please, I beg of you, again, have an open heart and mind as I share the following with each of you, what God has provided after much prayer and study.

Think back with me to what you've learned about the early church or the Temple of God back in Old Testament times, where the people were at odds with those who would try to influence them away from the true and living God, and to tempt them to worship their man-made god's. These were examples of god's *(small G)* which they could see and pray to and place within their homes. They had experienced how the true and living God had protected them in many ways and had provided those with a temple where they could worship and offer sacrifices to Him but there was still remained a drawing power towards these god's, or the idols of Satan. Does this sound familiar? How many times have you read of God's judgment against His people because of this sin? They would repent of their sin and turn back to God, but it wasn't long before they were drawn away by the power of Satan once again, seeking idol worship, a physical worship they could see, feel and even pray to.

The power of Satan and the desire he has to bias our belief in God hasn't changed. The world today is full of satanic gods and idols which serve his purpose in his attack on the children of God. So... how is Satan trying to get into 'our heads' as mentioned earlier?

It is my humble belief in the age in which we live; there is a throwback to the human need for a "concrete portrayal of God" which we can grasp hold of, something more to buttress our faith. Consider this possibility; an inward desire, not unlike that of God's chosen people when there was a demonstration of Himself to them during those early times. It was a physical as well as a spiritual demonstration. Remember Moses and the burning bush; the harsh times they had while in subjection to the Egyptians, and the plagues sent by God which assured their eventual freedom, including their trek through the desert for some 40 years where God fed them all during that time. There were countless situations where God's people saw and felt the living presence of God! What then, is the throwback today for a concrete portrayal of God for the Christian? You'll begin to see what the answer to this question is, as I provide a short history lesson on the much maligned "Word of God."

To begin with, I must provide the following understanding and clarification of biblical history as it relates to the errorless written scriptures, the Holy Bible, which has been handed down to us through the ages. A Book which was spoken into being through God selected writers who were the singular group which penned all of the original manuscripts.

All Scripture is God-breathed and is useful for teaching, rebuking, correcting and training in righteousness. (2 Timothy 3:16)

But let's stop now, and take a look at the English Bible in particular.

Since there's been a proliferation of English Bible translations as far back as AD 1382 starting with John Wycliffe's first complete *hand written* translation of the Bible from the Latin Vulgate into English. In our day and time, there has developed various schools of thought as to which version of God's Bible is the best from the accuracy perspective and as close to a 'word for word' translation as possible, in the time frame from which it was written.

Some, in relatively recent church leadership, have come to a decision and course of action, which I would characterize as; *"an un-biblical effort to <u>exclude</u> all who do not entertain the same choice of English translation as do they."*

In spite of this narrow judgment, there are others who enjoy reading various other alternate translations, which may be easier to understand, utilizing changes in English which have occurred over the last several hundred years to more clearly understand the contextual meaning of scripture. The exclusion attitude is held by those who have chosen to believe in the version, known as the KJV...or King James Version of 1611, re-edited in1615, 1629, 1638, 1762, and finally 1769, the version commonly used today.

This exclusion is not unlike what God's Bible teaches regarding the Pharisees of Jesus' day spoken of earlier, and the judgmental-ism they practiced. The undesired effect of taking this narrow view of scripture has been to drive many people away from the study of the Bible and even some from the church when attributing "God's inspiration" of this singular translation on a par with the original manuscripts! Most lay members in the church caught up in this, are simply *following the lead of local church leadership,* because the truth is, all people of God need to believe the Bible they read is the truthful source of the original scriptures. So, when their leadership invokes "Godly Inspiration" and a "Word for Word" translation like no other, while castigating all other translations... it does so, at the expense of displeasing God, and causing confusion in the Church Body at large.

Additionally, when people are dogmatic in this way about Bible selection, they seem to not be aware of the potential harm this sort of legalism is having on the growth of the church. God is not pleased with any man-made set of rules which flies in the face of His Grace to His children. Where this exclusionary doctrine is taught, it breeds an effective level of underlying displeasure or even hate, in place of love for fellow believers; albeit not necessarily blatant, but an undercurrent of judgmental-ism. *(God's Word is clear on the question of judging others! God only has the power and right to judge every situation!)*

But while all of this is going on, God who is in control, is watching, leading and, I believe, subtly making it profoundly clear to all, just what the real story is. It's all somewhat humorous based on the following! When the NKJV [New King James Version] hit the street, back in 1982, being commissioned in 1975, the diehard KJV proponents were in a tizzy! *What to do now...?* I seem to remember hearing of the scouring of this new version for anything which could be used to black list this reasonable effort to bring the language up-to-date, but... for the most part, their effort didn't grow legs.

Here's an example of a typical comparison of scripture.

Matthew 1:24-25

KJV... *Then Joseph being raised from sleep did as the angel of the Lord had bidden him, and took unto him his wife: And knew her not till she had brought forth her firstborn son: and he called his name JESUS.*

NKJV... *Then Joseph, being aroused from sleep, did as the angel of the Lord commanded him and took to him his wife, and did not know her till she had brought forth her firstborn Son. And he called His name JESUS.*

Now, compare these two to the NIV version.

NIV... *When Joseph woke up, he did what the angel of the Lord had commanded him and took Mary home as his wife. But he did not consummate their marriage until she gave birth to a son. And he gave him the name Jesus.*

Okay... the words have been changed, but the meaning is the same! When you read all three versions, are you bothered by the change in wording, or are they simply easier to understand? Is this a good thing? The purpose in making this distinction is just to say... It's a matter of choice, absolutely nothing more! One is as good as the other. *Here's why...*

Bible Scholars agree there are no *perfect grammatical translations* of the original manuscripts, due primarily to the real practical impossibilities of *100% word by word translation from one language to another.* To be sure, there most certainly are people who disagree with this truthful premise, but that's their choice. In any event, when the choice of translation evokes exclusion, or even disdain for anyone reading an alternate Bible version within a local Body of Christ, then this is a strong indication of "Worshiping a given Translation," rather than worshiping the "God *of* that translation," especially when the original translation has undergone several edition changes, and most certainly will never attain heavenly perfection in the sight of God! The key question; should I worship the Bible, or the God of the Bible, regardless of translation?

Answer: We worship God and Him only!

The following then, is how Satan works in answer to the "throwback question above."
"Could our worship of the Bible which we hold in our hands and read, and study, turn out to be effectively an

idol which we worship?" Think about that! When people are ready to fight and argue with other Christians about their belief in the King James Version of the Bible as the *only* God inspired Bible. Could it be that person's idol? Also, Satan finds a way for people to feed their pride even in the Scripture they read; even in the belief they hold regarding salvation. Imagine that... being prideful of the Bible you are holding in your hand, and also your very salvation, which if taken to the ultimate, may *only* be attained by the study of this *one particular* Bible, the King James Version! This may happen without the individual realizing it.

It's one thing to love the scriptures, the Bible, and quite another to worship it! Our worship should be exclusive only to God and nothing else. Any other worship is to *'idolize'* something, and that could well be a specific version of the Bible.

There is no doubt, this phenomenon is Satan driven, not God driven!

God seeks humility in His children, not pride! Again, if this attitude exists, does it not create brothers with the Pharisees of Jesus time?

Here's the truth in a nutshell... the good people of God have been blinded by this ungodly perspective of Bible translations. In keeping to this belief, those that do, promote a spirit of dissension, not love for one another. They promote a spirit of judgment which accomplishes the desires of Satan, not God. Paul, in his epistle to the Romans said;

"Do you not know that to whom you present yourselves slaves to obey, you are that one's slaves." (Romans 6:16) (KJV)

We are to submit ourselves to God as "slaves of God," not to church leaders or elders who have promoted this narrow view of scripture.

But now that you have been set free from sin and have become <u>slaves of God</u>, the benefit you reap leads to holiness, and the result is eternal life.
(Romans 6:22) (KJV) (Added emphasis)

We must make sure we aren't caught up in playing "follow the leader" out of shear unbiased ignorance to the truth which even the translators of the King James Version are also wanting you to understand is *faulty and even sinful*. Do not continue to put a "singular Bible version" on a pedestal! Submit only to the truth of God, and do not put the leadership of your church body on a pedestal as well, following blindly their every edict or teaching. We, individually, are responsible to God for *"rightly dividing the Word of truth."*

Study to shew thyself approved unto God, a workman that needeth not to be ashamed, rightly dividing the word of truth. (2 Timothy 2:15((KJV)

Even the KJV Bible today uses marginal references for certain words up-dated in today's English, or, in some cases, used in the NKJV, *(New King James Version)* in order to make the Bible more understandable. Here's an example...Matthew 16:3 KJV uses a word "lowering." In the margin, you can stop your reading and check out this word. But doing this interrupts your understanding of what you've read, so, you start all over again! By the way, the margin word is..."threatening." Isn't this the same as translating the Bible?

I ask... what's the big deal anyhow?

Here are the quotations including the NIV for comparative purposes;

Matthew 16:3

KJV *And in the morning, it will be foul weather today: for the sky is red and <u>lowering</u>...*

NKJV *And in the morning, 'It will be foul weather today, for the sky is red and <u>threatening</u>.*

NIV *And in the morning, 'Today it will be stormy, for the sky is red and <u>overcast</u>.*

Summation: "No translator or group of translators of God's Bible, has ever experienced the *direct distinction* of being "Inspired by God!" And this certainly includes the original translators of the King James Version.

There is but one inspired Canon of Scripture... the Original Manuscripts. To say otherwise, is to add a personal belief regarding scriptural development. Rev. 22:18-19 is again a warning to all who would take this path, by injecting personal and prideful faulty doctrine. There are those, as mentioned above, who call out *one translation* as the only God Inspired version of the Bible, and, in doing so, to effectively condemn and exclude all other English Bible versions." This is heresy of the highest order!

Here's the final and real truth of the matter!

Consider for a moment, the difficult task of translating scripture into English as well as the many different languages of the people of God the world over. If it wasn't for the tireless effort of many godly people, who have dedicated themselves to this task, the message of God would never have its potential place in the hearts of all mankind.

"The key focus of the translation process by men and women who love God and want to be as errorless as possible in their work, is to be sure that the words read and speak to the context of the subject matter, and that each word is grammatically as correct as possible as well as the differences such as pronoun use from one language to another." There are numerous additional translation considerations which must be followed to insure against error.

The efforts by those wonderful translators back in the early 1600's, which penned the King James Version, did not consider what they accomplished as *inspired of God*, but rather, it was the "Inspired Word" they used to transfer meaning from the original language into the English of their day. It's as simple as that!

May I also say the use of the KJV as the desired version for church worship, is certainly not in question here, as viable scripture. In fact, the church I presently attend has historically used this version for worship and teaching. A choice not driven by any perceived scriptural superiority by church leadership, but a church which acknowledges the inspiration of the original writers. The choice of which Bible to use, is for each church to decide.

From the time I was a child, I was taught from the KJV. It was through these years I began to discover a sort of segregation in believers, which in my mind and heart was troublesome; segregation not unlike that of race. Indeed, the two seemed to emanate from the same mindset, driven from a superiority position. Most, if not all of these churches, also resisted allowing church membership to people of color, in particular our black brothers. This was when God began to speak to me about the lack of humility and love for *all* believers, I was experiencing in the church. Something was all wrong! Something was amiss in a huge way. When I went off to the Army, I knew I was given the command to live a life filled with an open heart to learn the truth. And wouldn't you know it... God cemented this concern in my heart by having me be the only white person in my barracks for over a year! I quickly experienced a direct compassioned understanding of what "exclusion" was all about! I made numerous trips to Detroit carrying my African American brother's home. I was invited into their homes as a brother, not a white boy! In many indelible ways I saw what life was all about from the black perspective. It was not a pretty sight!

This book is the exposé of what I've learned. *(Now, back to the narrative)*

Are there those in churches like the above which hold to the inspiration of the KJV as the only God inspired translation? No doubt about it, and there are also different levels of adherence to this view of Bible translation. Some are extremely adamant, and some have rarely, if ever thought about it, thus it is incumbent on the church to make clear what might be called, the "bibliolatry" of belief, or the idolatrous error of this view of Bible translation. To not come to grips with this oftentimes hidden sin in the church, flies in the face of scripture.

Here we hear the words of Jesus;

You study the Scriptures diligently because <u>you think that in "them" you have eternal life</u>. These are the very Scriptures that testify about me, yet you refuse to come to me to have life. (John 5: 39-40) (Added emphasis)

Jesus knew the fallacy of the Pharisees and their personal idolatry of scripture, embellished with their own set of legalistic beliefs which blinded them from seeing Jesus for who He truly was. This same narrow view which some hold of the KJV is no different. We are to believe the Bible by our faith in God, not by our faith in one singular translation. This is not a Bible or Scripture issue...it's a translation issue, therefore, to not teach against the potential for this kind of translation idolatry is to not teach the whole of faith.

... and everything that does not come from faith is sin. (Romans 14:23)

When undercurrents of known sin are allowed to continue unabated, for fear of some negative impact on the church if brought to light, is to take on God's responsibility for the results of teaching truth. Just to let *"sleeping dogs lie"* is to effectively remove God from the equation.

Those in leadership faced with this potential sin in their church, must not be fearful of preaching and teaching the truth. They should not, *any longer*, take a politically expedient approach to a patently wrong non-doctrinal issue, and allow it to be a "real doctrinal issue" in the minds of some of the people.

In spite of these human difficulties and intricacies of grammatical decision making in the translation process, God has instructed all of His children to...

And he said unto them, Go ye into all the world, and preach the gospel to every creature. (Mark 16:15) (KJV)

God has proven to be the God of all creation. He has proven who He is by the simple reality of His Living Word, the Holy Bible, which has withstood every assault man and Satan could muster. No other book written by man has ever, or will ever come close to the propagation of His never dying sacred writings. To put it in terms understandable to us humans today... God is the greatest Marketer of Truth the Universe has ever known. His church is indestructible! His method of birthing human beings into His Family is clearly understood in spite of man's limited ability to perfectly join one word after another into a perfect representation of what God would write as the real Author of His Word.

Friends and fellow believers, God "breathed" His inspired scripture through the original writers over a time frame of some 1500 plus calendar years.

148

All Scripture is <u>God-breathed</u> and is useful for teaching, rebuking, correcting and training in righteousness (2 Timothy 3:16) (Added emphasis)

And, I might add, all who have followed have come to faith in Him in the same way, by His simple plan of salvation. It was through these original inspired writers, God provided His inerrant, never dying Bible.

The work of biblical translation is not finished. There are still many languages and dialects around the world which need the scriptures translated for the people to become aware of Jesus Christ and His salvation message. We should be praying for this effort to continue as God has commanded. The argument discussed above loses all meaning when you consider the KJV cannot be understood by many of the people on this planet, simply because they do not speak English. What about these people? How will they come to the knowledge of Jesus Christ?

Additionally, the Holy Spirit of God is at work constantly in this world regardless of the specific scripture one reads. The Holy Spirit as the third person of the Trinity, is convicting, prompting, leading and making Himself evident to believers in an untold multitude of ways too numerous to mention. In spite of the satanic power we are forced to deal with, God, through His Spirit, provides each of His children with victory over Satan!

Now, let's put all of this into perspective!

Think of it! A lowly poor couple, not yet given in marriage, giving birth to the Son of the Living God! A baby boy which would not live as a human being passed the age of 33 years, but one who would experience resurrection and ultimate transfiguration and ascension to be with His Father in Glory! His unimaginable impact on the world is still underway, not stopped by man or Satan. The Holy Son of God throughout time and eternity! *We are privileged one day soon to stand in His presence in humility and love!*

What Bible version we read while here on earth... will not matter!

In concluding this short historical reality of what has happened in the church regarding the development of readable Scripture, I've decided to use the NIV version for the bulk of the references in this book, for the precise reason of making God's story come alive to all who are impressed to want to read the book. If you're interested in exploring the historical development of this Bible translation, published by Zondervan Publishing House and Tyndale House Publishers Inc., you can find it in the front of their "Life Application Study Bible," where they have provided almost 2 1/2 pages covering the details of how the NIV Bible came into being. Additionally, you'll note as you read, I've used a number of different Bible versions to provide clarity and better understanding of God's direction for our lives.

"Holiness"

As God is Holy, so we are to be Holy!

You, the LORD said to Moses, "Speak to the entire assembly of Israel and say to them: 'Be holy because I, the LORD your God, am holy.'" "Each of you must respect his mother and father, and you must observe my Sabbaths. I am the LORD your God. Do not turn to idols or make gods of cast metal for yourselves. I am the LORD your God." (Leviticus 19:1–4)

The Apostle Peter amplified this in *(1 Peter 1:15-16)*

But just as he who called you is holy, so be holy in all you do; for it is written: "Be holy, because I am holy."

People are holy when they are devoted to God, and separated from sin. When sin is detested, we become acceptable to God by Christ's death and our acceptance of this reality. Our sins are gone; past, present and future, if we honestly listen to the Holy Spirit when He touches our heart, and telling us to seek Jesus. When we forget about ourselves, and begin to think about others, and their needs, we are moving towards a greater degree of holiness. God is now pleased with us and has good reason to shower blessings in our direction.

In the book of Hebrews, the writer brings together the practicality of the New Covenant, against the old Law. *(Abrahamic Covenant)*

The writer, which many believe to be the Apostle Paul, speaks in language applicable for all time. The amazing words you are about to read, clarifies beyond description, the difference between Old and New Testament times.

This is an illustration for the present time, indicating that the gifts and sacrifices being offered were not able to clear the conscience of the worshiper. They are only a matter of food and drink and various ceremonial washings—external regulations applying until the time of the new order.

When Christ came as high priest of the good things that are already here, he went through the greater and more perfect tabernacle that is not man-made, that is to say, not a part of this creation. He did not enter by means of the blood of goats and calves; but he entered the Most Holy Place once for all by his own blood, having obtained eternal redemption.

The blood of goats and bulls and the ashes of a heifer sprinkled on those who are ceremonially unclean sanctify them so that they are outwardly clean. How much more, then, will the blood of Christ, who through the eternal Spirit offered himself unblemished to God, cleanse our consciences from acts that lead to death, so that we may serve the living God! For this reason Christ is the mediator of a new covenant, that those who are called, may receive the promised eternal inheritance—now that he has died as a ransom to set them free from the sins committed under the first covenant. (Hebrews 9:9-15)

Therefore, Holiness is the attribute of God which we are instructed to seek. As born again children, we will be drawn to God, but... while still in the flesh, Satan attempts to overpower this relationship by temptation. "We will fail, but God will prevail!" Our future is secure, but our life on earth may be plagued by the results of our continuing ability and penchant to sin. There is always a price to pay for wrong doing. God does not tempt us in any way, but Satan is constantly after the believer as part of his battle with Christ. He has been at it since the world came into being. Just look back at the people of God, the Jews. They were just like a YoYo. Sinning, and then repenting! This was repeated constantly, but God did not give up on them. He judged them over and over! Their opportunities for future restoration are in the hands of God. It will happen! *More to come on this, later in the book!*

"Are Answers really Answers?"

Have you ever met someone, who when asked a question, always has the answer? This person seems never to be befuddled. Never do you hear something like this from them... "I don't know," or, "I've wondered about that myself."

Some, like the person above, seem to have a need to be seen as knowledgeable, or at least to have some kind of an answer, be it opinion or hopefully truth. This is the same person spoken of earlier, which repeatedly butts in on your conversation not allowing you to finish what you had in mind to say to them. We all need to consider this question in light of God's desire for "humility" in our lives. Have you ever uttered this phrase...? "I don't know?" If you have a hard time remembering the last time you heard these words escaping your mouth, then you may need to consider your typical responses. Are they driven by a seeming need to demonstrate superior knowledge?

Do people like this exist? Yes they do, otherwise, why the obvious statement... "He, or she is a "know it all!" God is not honored, nor do we have the opportunity to honor Him to others if they lack respect for us. Respect flows from humility. Humility flows from an honest evaluation of self. On the other hand, pride flows from being a "know it all!" All of us are susceptible. Consider the following Scripture;

"I, wisdom, dwell together with prudence; I possess knowledge and discretion. To fear the LORD is to hate evil; I hate pride and arrogance, evil behavior and per-verse speech. Counsel and sound judgment are mine; I have understanding and power." (Proverbs 8:12-14)

Here, "wisdom" speaks about hating evil, pride, and arrogance, including perverse speech. Implied in the Scripture is the reality of humility which all of us that walk with Christ should exhibit to others. It also speaks of the need to be a good listener as opposed to being a controller of all conversation. People like this, may wonder why others are not comfortable around them. There's another Scripture which speaks to the need for being a good listener.

My dear brothers, take note of this: Everyone should be quick to listen, slow to speak.... (James 1:18)

"Do not despair... I am There"

Earthquakes, tornadoes, floods, drunk drivers, assassins, fearful situations, in a world overflowing with all kinds of evil including the loss of a President by who knows who? Where is God? Is he impotent? Millions of people have been plagued by the ongoing flow of the result of sin. No one, including the Christian is exempt! There is overwhelming despair in all of this, but this need not be. Losses in life are sometimes overwhelming, but for the Christian there is no room for despair.

Twenty-five centuries ago, one of God's choicest of all servants, a man named Daniel, had many reasons to despair since he and thousands of his countrymen were shipped off to a foreign land as the result of being conquered by the enemy. You most likely know the story, about Daniel and his three friends Hananiah, Mishael and Azariah, otherwise known as Shadrach, Meshach and Abednego. By this time, all three of them held important positions within the Babylonian government. The unfolding of the story results in all of them being thrown into a huge blazing furnace because they refused to bow to the King's wishes. But, when King Nebuchadnezzar looked down into the furnace he saw four men standing there and came away knowing that God was with them. *(Daniel 3)* This historical account proves the fact that these three men did not despair because they knew God was there!

A good definition of despair, is simply "giving up." It's man's way of pouting like a child who doesn't get what he or she wants. The essence of despair is... "not having our way!" We sometimes use despair as a cover for a lack of faith. From God's perspective, it is the reverse of faith. This attitude of heart and mind can lead to deep depression. So quitting is patently dangerous, wouldn't you say? It's also a refusal to seek God. It's a demonstration of wanting pity, seeking attention, while forcefully wanting to draw others down and make them feel your pain, all the while seeking your sympathy. When you see this in others do not sympathize with them. That's what they want. Rather, "empathize" with them.

I once heard a very convincing story of the difference between sympathy and empathy. Envision yourself on a cruise with a friend when a storm arose and many begin to get seasick including your friend. He stood at the railing up- chucking all of that wonderful food! Now, if you were "sympathetic" to him, you would end up doing the same thing he was doing. On the other hand, if you are empathetic, you would try to get him to the center of the boat... right in the very middle where there is hardly any movement at all of the boat, other than up and down. Two distinctively different frames of mind we can have when someone needs our help, being sympathetic shows concern and compassion without much help, while empathy also shows compassion, but with much help.

God understands our penchant for despair. But when we make Him ours, it's a word and a frame of mind we dispose of as quickly as possible by not giving up and in turn, seeking God.

"Categorizing People"

Did Jesus do this? This common occurrence is what old world Englishmen would call... "Dastardly." It's an insidious judgment of people which are not to our liking. The telling indication of this spiritual malady is when we discuss with others our feelings about so-and-so. Finding our "Place in Society," some would say.

It's the process of segregating ourselves from others. Have you ever said, something like... "He (or she) drives me crazy!" I believe we are all guilty, aren't we? But, is God happy with this general attitude of life? I think not. I ask again; did Jesus do this?

Whether you're black, brown, yellow, white, or even green... with envy... you're all the same to God! Whether you're dirty, clean, smelly, sick or healthy... it makes no difference to God! So, the question becomes for each one of us as His children, am I guilty of not being as much like the Savior as I should? Jesus was all things to all people. We should try to emulate that attitude with everyone we come in contact with. It's true that close friendships usually occur between people that are like-minded in some way. Jesus was no different in that His disciples were close to Him in ways not enjoyed by the general public. It's also true that they were all chosen for a specific purpose not just friendship. But in spite of the results of sin in everyone's life which deemed most to be undesirable, Jesus still loved each one with the same amount of love and concern.

The very person you may have disdain for, might also be the very person Jesus is calling into your life for some specific purpose. This being true, here's an idea that God has prompted me with while thinking through this whole subject matter. When meeting someone new, or even someone not too likable, visualize the face of Jesus when looking into their eyes. You cannot look at the face of Jesus without a smile on your face, can you? When attempting to treat anyone we meet, just as if that person were Jesus Christ, we exchange the negative to the positive. We are attempting to stand in the shoes of our Savior. If you'll honestly make an effort to react to people in this way, you will be amazed at what you will learn about people that otherwise you would be blind to. Opportunities to be a witness of the saving grace of Jesus Christ will come your way, much more than you ever thought possible. God expects His children to be clean in their heart towards others. It's a responsibility we should not take lightly, and we should disavow our natural human inclinations of segregation. "Nuff said!"

"What are You?"

S ome may both think and say, "My value in the body of Christ isn't very much, if anything!" Not true! Paul clearly made sure in 1 Corinthians, that all of God's children are particularly useful in their sphere of influence. Take the time to read this portion of Scripture out loud.

Even so the body is not made up of one part but of many. Now if the foot should say, "Because I am not a hand, I do not belong to the body," it would not for that reason stop being part of the body. And if the ear should say, "Because I am not an eye, I do not belong to the body," it would not for that reason stop being part of the body. If the whole body were an eye, where would the sense of hearing be? If the whole body were an ear, where would the sense of smell be? But in fact God has placed the parts in the body, every one of them, just as he wanted them to be. If they were all one part, where would the body be? As it is, there are many parts, but one body. The eye cannot say to the hand, "I don't need you!" And the head cannot say to the feet, "I don't need you!" On the contrary, those parts of the body that seem to be weaker are indispensable, and the parts that we think are less honorable we treat with special honor. And the parts that are unpresentable are treated with special modesty, while our presentable parts need no special treatment. But God has put the body together, giving greater honor to the parts that lacked it, so that there should be no division in the body, but that its parts should have equal con-

cern for each other. If one part suffers, every part suffers with it; if one part is honored, every part rejoices with it. (1 Corinthians 12:14–26)

In this scriptural analogy, God has made sure to include everyone, in the work required to be accomplished. The importance of each Christian can only be measured by God. That being true, we all must be careful not to walk on either side of the fence. What do you mean by that Bob? Well, some feel totally unimportant while others tend to want the spotlight. Some are overly entranced by their education *(the mind)*. Some tend to toot their own horn *(the talker)*. Some have all the answers *(the mouth)*.

These are but a few of the potential pitfalls, we as servants of God fall into. We also tend to stroke our talents with prideful thoughts of power and control, while sanctimoniously giving God the credit for *"my wonderful opportunity to serve God like no one else!"* Do you think I'm exaggerating a little bit here? Question, have you ever, for even one split second, thought more highly of yourself than you ought, or less highly than you should?

Either side of the fence is sinful and not pleasing to God. Stay away from the fence, and allow God to be seen in you through humility and love. "A haughty spirit" is displeasing to God. Are you more satisfied with yourself than with God? Remember... your life is meaningless without God. Self-sufficiency is a major error in our thinking process. Go to God with the smallest of details. Continually seek His direction in all things.

"Claiming the Shoes of Others"

God instructs us to pray and have honest concern for others, seeking in every way possible to understand their plight and all of the difficulties they are faced with. By putting their shoes on, metaphorically, we seek to know and feel their pain. In doing so, we are better able to meet some of their needs. We need to also remember that all we have belongs to God. That being true, we need to seek His guidance in what, how and where He wants us to give and help others. He "gave" Himself for us! We are instructed to "give" ourselves to others. Forget the cost! God will provide. This is nothing more or less than Christianity in action.

When we put on their shoes, and demonstrate honest service and humility towards them, a doorstop has been placed under their hearts door providing a God driven opportunity to share the love of Christ to them. Now, the Holy Spirit is in control. Love and joy start to flow simultaneously like never before! There is no greater challenge for the Christian than to be used of Him in a way to change the heart and life of another child of God. Praise God from whom all blessings flow!

"Physical Corruption"

"Bodily sin, disguised as pleasure, but filled with an ungodly appetite for lust and ultimate destruction by the hand of God."

That's a good definition of physical corruption. Sin of this sort, is a marriage between Satan and fallen man. It's physical gratification run amok! The difference between an animal and God's chosen, "In His image" children, the highest order of physical life, is that of having a Spirit. The Spirit of man, because of original sin, has been "corrupted" and can only be cleansed by the Holy Spirit of God, through God's unbelievable sacrifice of His Son, Jesus Christ! Our world today, is no different than what Hosea and the prophets of God experienced, where the people were living like animals who only know one way to respond to their physical appetites. The animals are driven in a comparative senseless manner. There is no right and wrong to them. What they're about is "survival." Each life is extended at the cost of another life. We call this simply… the natural order of animal life, not realizing the fact that even the animal kingdom was corrupted by the fall of man. The loss of a "perfect" sinless world through man's disobedience created corruption! This is a physical and spiritual state, which will only end in eternal death and separation from God, the Creator.

We take all of this for granted. To think that it could have been different is just incomprehensible. Any view to the contrary, is like searching for the pot of gold at the end of the rainbow! It's a utopia! It's not possible! Its senseless most feel, so we continue through life acting out the lifestyle of our animal kingdom in our own "dog-eat-dog" world just one step above the senseless life of pure animal destruction. We try to "marry" right over wrong, by the development of the legal system of justice and so-called order. When in truth, violation of the system is commonplace. We try to be "good," but find it difficult, if not impossible. We wonder why some are not able to navigate life and become mentally deranged. There is this constant plight in seeking to be truthful, while living unlawfully and when failure continues to be present. We are simply "corrupted!" That is, corrupted by sin. Jails are full, mental hospitals are full, "fear" rules our lives. Peace is temporary at best, and of course, all of this is curable with money, fame and fortune. *Yeah right!*

Some try as they may to live above all of this, driven by desire for right instead of wrong, but it is next to impossible. Solomon, in all of his wisdom, characterized life… For what it really is… Nothing more than "deadly corruption" destined for death, not life. But, God loved this fallen world of His making, too much to allow it to remain controlled by sin and the father of it... Satan. God, through His Word has promised to once and for all destroy sin and Satan and to reconstruct a "new heaven and a new earth," a place where sin is nonexistent, where He is in complete control. No longer will His children be driven by "blind desire at the expense of others," but by the new desire to conform to the image and will of God.

Ironically, we, even in this present condition of life, have the opportunity to step inside, as it were, the heavily lifestyle of the promised future, but in a limited manner. God through the sacrifice of Jesus and the promises of His future kingdom offers us a small glimpse of the future. We can experience His presence in these sinful bodies. We can "see" into the future by simply accepting His plan of change. A change we call salvation, the reality of being literally saved from eternal damnation caused by corruption, the result of original sin.

The choice is ours to accept or reject... to exit this life of sin, or to remain in the presence of Satan, "taking our chances" in this "dog eat dog" sin-driven world.

Are you going to allow the "lust of the flesh" control your destiny, or are you willing to repent of sin and be changed by God? A one-time change! An eternal change back to what God wanted us to be. It's His grace we can thank for this opportunity to stand in the presence of God Almighty with a clean conscience, and never again to witness the kind of corruption that we see in this world today.

"God's Holy Tissue"

One morning while coming to the close of Bible study and time of prayer, the prayer list I was holding

161

in my hand, inadvertently caught the edge of an old wound on the back of my left hand, in a minor way, but it wasn't long before blood began to appear once again. I grabbed a tissue from the drawer of an adjacent table, and took the edge of the tissue to soak up the small drop of blood which had appeared. I did this several times, until the design of a loving God took over and the blood ceased from flowing. "God is the one responsible for the simple, but profound healing process." He sealed the wound to allow for the healing process to continue.

Prior to this simple experience at the conclusion of my prayer time, while I was sipping the remainder of my coffee, I looked over at my notepad and wondered why several days had passed without hearing the explicit voice of God instructing me to write. Then the above took place. The prayer list, on that piece of paper, now took on a whole new meaning for me. It was Jesus reminding me to take note of His redeeming blood, which was the center of my salvation.

He accepted His father's call to be wounded for our sin... Paying the penalty for that sin on the cross so many years ago. God used His Heavenly Tissue to seal up the wounds He suffered, and in doing so sealed up our sin never to be seen or heard of again, but only if we choose to "believe" in the reality of His purpose in coming to earth, as the only Son of God to be our personal Redeemer.

He was the "God man." The singular life God provided as payment to save us from eternal damnation. It was the "tissue" of His life and death which "sealed" our redemption. Thank you dear Jesus!

"Nine and Ten"

In reading, and studying the Bible, there are times when discovery of how uniquely this book was put together pop up and grab our attention. While studying the book of Zechariah, God brought the following to mind. These two verses exemplify the twin coming of Jesus Christ. One is the promised Savior, and the second as the King of heaven. This prophecy was over 500 years old before Jesus, as Matthew 21: 1–11 tells us, of His triumphal entry into Jerusalem... Specifically verses 9–10. Then in Philippians 2: 9–10 God's Word foretells the coming reality that every knee will bow to Christ and every tongue will confess Him as the eternal Lord.

Here, I believe, is shown the practicality of God, even in helping us remember these truths. I can find no specific significance and why Zechariah 9: 9–10, Matthew 2: 9–10, Philippians 2: 9–10 and lest we forget... The central key to our salvation, Romans 10: 9–10 all speak in concert of the written truth of God's plan of salvation, His ultimate long-range purpose for His chosen people, including its expansion into a world of believers.

Now, believers in God, from His birth as the Son, through His triumphal entry into the Holy City..., and then, at the chosen precise future moment in time, His final return to the New Earth as Lord and Master of the universe will take place to the consternation of many, and the most joyous moment in all of history to those who have chosen their eternal future; a coming, undeniable future with God.

God's message... encapsulated for us in a way for us to easily remember. Here are the above Scriptures in the order given for your enjoyment!

(Zechariah 9: 9-10)
Rejoice greatly, O Daughter of Zion! Shout, Daughter of Jerusalem! See, your king comes to you, righteous and having salvation, gentle and riding on a donkey, on a colt, the foal of a donkey. I will take away the chariots from Ephraim and the war-horses from Jerusalem, and

the battle bow will be broken. He will proclaim peace to the nations. His rule will extend from sea to sea and from the River to the ends of the earth.

(Matthew 21: 9-10)
The crowds that went ahead of him and those that followed shouted, "Hosanna to the Son of David!" "Blessed is he who comes in the name of the Lord!" "Hosanna in the highest!" When Jesus entered Jerusalem, the whole city was stirred and asked, "Who is this?"

(Philippians 2: 9-10)
Therefore God exalted him to the highest place and gave him the name that is above every name, that at the name of Jesus every knee should bow, in heaven and on earth and under the earth...

(Romans 10: 9-10)
That if you confess with your mouth, "Jesus is Lord," and believe in your heart that God raised him from the dead, you will be saved. For it is with your heart that you believe and are justified, and it is with your mouth that you confess and are saved.

I would not be surprised if there would be additional places in Scripture where 9 and 10 are additional parts of the puzzle. Check it out, and let me know!

"All will Know!"

One day soon... The disdain and rejection of Jesus Christ, as the one and only Messiah, will be vindicated. Not by destruction, but by love and compassion from God His father for His chosen people. All of the people of God, all of the Jewish nation in particular, and all of the Saints, both then and now who have called on the name of Jesus as Savior and Lord, will know once and for all time, that Jesus is indeed, the crucified Messiah.

His chosen people will no longer toss Jesus aside as a false Messiah. Quite the opposite, they will mourn for him. Every man woman and child of the nation of Israel, will go into private mourning for the one "they" as a nation pierced and killed, and then for thousands of years have rejected as their King and Messiah. Their eyes will be opened to the truth, as will the eyes of the entire world.

This truth is why the Hallelujah Chorus was written. It's why many were burned at the stake. And, why millions who have spent a lifetime of rejection, because of their faithful worship and unending love for the Son of God. It's why this book, and thousands more like it, have been written with the eternal hope of one more person honestly coming to grips with their personal sin, and then, to take the step of inviting God into their heart and life by the acceptance of the sacrifice of God's Son Jesus Christ. Listen as Zechariah, Paul and John all come together with a verbal painting of the end times, which we believe, is just around the corner!

(Zechariah 12: 10-14)
"And I will pour out on the house of David and the inhabitants of Jerusalem a spirit of grace and supplication. They will look on me, the one they have pierced, and they will mourn for him as one mourns for an only child, and grieve bitterly for him as one grieves for a firstborn son. On that day the weeping in Jerusalem will be great, like the weeping of Hadad Rimmon in the plain of Megiddo. The land will mourn, each clan by itself, with their wives by themselves: the clan of the house of David and their wives, the clan of the house of Nathan and their wives, the clan of the house of Levi and their wives, the clan of

Shimei and their wives, and all the rest of the clans and their wives.

(Philippians 2: 9-11)
Therefore God exalted him to the highest place and gave him the name that is above every name, that at the name of Jesus every knee should bow, in heaven and on earth and under the earth, and every tongue confess that Jesus Christ is Lord, to the glory of God the Father.

(Revelation 5: 13)
Then I heard every creature in heaven and on earth and under the earth and on the sea, and all that is in them, singing:
"To him who sits on the throne and to the Lamb be praise and honor and glory and power, for him and him ever and ever!"

One day soon… "All will know!" Where are you located in this picture?

"Who is Wise?"

This age-old question is doubtless one of the most important thoughts to consider. It's not for us to consider wisdom as a goal to be obtained, but rather as a result of simple and profound obedience to God. The real and better question is; who is Wisdom?

Listen now with your heart at what Hosea, a remarkable prophet of God to His people Ephraim *(Israel)* has to say at the very end of his book.

(Hosea 14: 9)
Who is wise? He will realize these things. Who is discerning? He will understand them. The ways of the LORD

are right; the righteous walk in them, but the rebellious stumble in them.

Wise and discerning people walk in the light. They allow the God of the universe to direct their paths. They "see", because of His light, not their own. To walk in our own light is to walk in darkness.

(Proverbs 4: 19) spells it out for us.
But the way of the wicked is like deep darkness; they do not know what makes them stumble.

In my study, I discovered a godly formula for wisdom in chapter 2 of Proverbs. I discovered the need to keep walking in His light. It's nothing more than a simple multiplication formula...

3 x 4 = 12.
3 = Conditions, the word... *if.*
x = Transition, the word... *then.*
4 = the Provider, the words... *His & He.*
12 = His statement of truth and promised results, the word... *will.*

Now, don't get caught up in the formula, but it is interesting to note that

Conditions *times* God *equals* Promises.

This mathematical reality is not coincidental. We're to focus on the conditions, then, God will provide the necessary wisdom we need.
Again, I strongly suggest you read this scripture passage OUT LOUD! It reinforces your understanding by employing the sound of your voice, in addition to your mental hearing. Once you get used to reading in this manner, you'll be hooked, I guarantee!

(Proverbs Chapter 2)
*My son, **if** you accept my words and store up my commands within you, turning your ear to wisdom and applying your heart to understanding, and **if** you call out for insight and cry aloud for understanding, and **if** you look for it as for silver and search for it as for hidden treasure, **then** you will understand the fear of the LORD and find the knowledge of God. For the LORD gives wisdom, and from **his** mouth come knowledge and understanding **He** holds victory in store for the upright, **he** is a shield to those whose walk is blameless, for **he** guards the course of the just and protects the way of his faithful ones. **Then** you **will** understand what is right and just and fair— every good path. For wisdom **will** enter your heart and knowledge **will** be pleasant to your soul. Discretion **will** protect you, and understanding **will** guard you. Wisdom **will** save you from the ways of wicked men, from men whose words are perverse, who leave the straight paths to walk in dark ways, who delight in doing wrong and rejoice in the perverseness of evil, whose paths are crooked and who are devious in their ways. It **will** save you also from the adulteress, from the wayward wife with her seductive words, who has left the partner of her youth and ignored the covenant she made before God. For her house leads down to death and her paths to the spirits of the dead. None who go to her return or attain the paths of life. Thus you **will** walk in the ways of good men and keep to the paths of the righteous. For the upright **will** live in the land, and the blameless **will** remain in it; but the wicked **will** be cut off from the land, and the unfaithful **will** be torn from it.*
(Added emphasis)

Clearly, God expects His children to daily seek for His wisdom. He's told us how, so there's nothing stopping us except US!

"Crumble or Live?"

Ask anyone whether they want to live or die, and the answer is, they want to live. Aside from a possible mental affliction, no one wants to die. Witness the immense fight someone, with the dreaded disease of cancer puts up. They will spend their last dime, and even go into debt to "beat" this often called terminal sickness.

Why then do people reject, out of hand, the opportunity to live forever? They may follow a mechanical religion simply out of duty, but not out of a faithful acceptance and belief in God. The answer lies in a mindless acceptance of the deceit (sin) of Satan. Pure and simple, his influence from the moment of his appearance to Adam and Eve is an eternal life-threatening reality bent on blinding the minds and hearts of all who will not listen to the message of truth. People who are caught up in following blindly their natural... from birth bent towards sin and deceit.

Although death is inevitable, most will not seek to learn the truth about eternal life with our maker. Thus the cryptic statement... "If there is a hell, I'll have a lot of friends there!" As if that will make it all okay! It all goes back to the attitude of... "No one is going to tell me what to do!" What they miss is that statement is right out of the mouth of Satan! No one will argue that there is evil in this world, and few think much about where it all came from... They either just put up with it, or they are guilty of promoting it because of their own evil inclinations. As we have discussed earlier, Satan is the antithesis of Jesus Christ, and there is an ongoing battle between the forces of God and the forces of evil which are linked to Satan, but all still under the control of God!. In the mind of God back in the beginning, His purpose was to allow this satanic rule to exist. He has allowed Satan to be the tempter, as was true in the oldest book in the Bible, the story of Job. As you study this wonderful book, you will soon learn about the temptation to sin and to turn your back on God. Just as the Old Testament law provided the knowledge of good and evil, as well as teaching the need for obedience to God and God only, it paved the way for a better testament, the New Testament resulting in the plan of God for a way of redemption for all of His children. *With the above in mind,*

One day Satan will crumble! And will take many with him. What's your choice? Crumble or live?

"Terminal, what Is... and what Isn't?"

Terminal... What we find when we arrive at the end of our road, or journey. In every large city there usually is a plane, train and bus terminal. "The road to the city ends at the terminal, it's been said." It's also a place where the individual arrives home or possibly just a stopping over connection point on the road home. It's a hub, a destination for some and a pause for others. It's a word for expressing the end of it all, or at least we may think it's the end, as in the phrase; "Terminal Cancer or terminal loss of Brain Function." You get the idea. We often make the judgment of another person's life, when we say... looks like a terminal disease! We find this okay, based on the mere percentage of people which die at the hand of such an ugly, so-called "terminal" disease. A malady for which mankind has not yet discovered a cure. We find ourselves in a hopeless state, when the doctor informs us personally of an incurable disease. The finish line is now somewhat visible. But what we've always known could happen, is now measurable to a degree.

Terminal: "a word with many meanings, all of which point to the end of a journey."

But, dear friend, as a believer in God, there should be no fear. Rather, our worst fear should be replaced by pure joy for what we are about to behold will confirm our life purpose... That is to love and serve our blessed Savior, with the knowledge that the word "Terminal" will be stricken from our vocabulary and replaced with "Eternal," a never ending life with God!

"Just Words, Hmmm? - No Way!"

God knows all things! What a statement to consider. It's a declaration of His "Omniscience," His all-knowing Godly attribute. Whether a believer in Christ or one who has decided to reject Him, He still knows everything about you! When you think about it... what a great question to ask someone God has prompted you to speak to about His salvation gift. Allow me to spell out an example... *"Jake, is there anyone who knows everything about you?"* Thought-provoking? You bet! The typical answer usually will be; "Probably only God."

To cement this truth in the mind of the apparent unbeliever, share with them the following Scripture.

Nothing in all creation is hidden from God's sight. Everything is uncovered and laid bare before the eyes of Him to whom we must give account. (Hebrews 4: 13)

Then go back and show them verse 12.

For the word of God is living and active. Sharper than any double-edged sword, it penetrates even to dividing soul and spirit, joints and marrow; it judges the thoughts and attitudes of the heart.

Continuing... out of this experience, the thunderous reality that the Book of God, the Bible, is not just another book. Not just an historical document or storybook of ancient times. No, a million times no. It is living! It has the power to put all of us on our knees. It cuts deeply into our ungodly actions and attitudes. It is like an artist who, when watched intently, starts with a blank sheet of parchment and slowly begins to tell a living story of life. With each passing stroke of the brush, the many colors and shading starts to become alive with meaning and purpose... until, and as you consider, and are captured by this living story in the making, you can hardly wait to view the completed picture. My friend, that's the "Word of God!"

You are the picture! God is the artist! The Bible: Just words? No way!

"Senior Power"

The truth of human frailty must not be overlooked. As our mind and intellect begin to lose strength... the loss of memory, the inability to connect the important with the unimportant, the limited desire for considering the future, while falling prey to both the physical and mental, and, an ever-increasing reality of our self-worth. There is no doubt that this occurs as we enter those last years of our life

Opposing these obvious conditions of age, we as believers, gain many new and powerful insights from a more direct connection to God than ever thought possible! Does God speak in ways which our language calls wisdom or a sort of piling up of historical events and experiences? I think otherwise! My heart and mind have come to believe in the entrance of the Holy Spirit into God's senior servants minds *(intellect)* and hearts *(place of compassion)* exhibiting His message uniquely to others in various ways too powerful to fully describe. It's more than just a long experience of living... its God at work preparing each of his children, as they uniquely take on a godly role in life which they never expected!

Some might postulate... With time available and a declining need to focus on making a living, God uses this time of life in a creative and needed way to advance His plan for adding individuals into His family. Could be... I guess... but only He is privy to this possible reality. Only He is able to make it happen. Only He can interject this unique life changing purpose His plan requires. Time and eternity will bring to light a significant birthing process within the lives of seniors not fully understood, and overlooked by those not yet part of the process. Indeed, those who have not yet reached this time of life do not realize the power afforded by God to these, His chosen older people to accomplish His goals.

If only younger people could think clearly about the reality of this power made available to our senior citizens!

In order to help this thought process, allow me to share some of the contributing factors in the obvious plan of God tied directly to Senior Power.

Obviously the first thing to consider, as mentioned above, is the availability of time! The senior child of God, *(that's a reality, not an oxymoron)* has attained the frame of mind of the absolute value of studying the word of God. Those which take advantage of the time available have contributed much to our society and God's church. You read many stories I'm sure, about senior citizens finishing up their education with many wondering why an earth would they want to do that! I won't go into detail now, regarding specifics concerning these different kinds of contributions, but they are many and varied. Many children have been influenced by grandparents who have shared their lives and have made an indelible impression on them.

Secondly, various opportunities for service in the church and other useful organizations in society are

filled by senior citizens who still have much to contribute. Upon reaching this age bracket, personal ego
loses its power over the individual and is replaced by
a new and more honest attitude of self worth. Because
of this truth, people will perform jobs and make themselves available for things younger people would consider beneath their dignity. This speaks to the humility
and God given power to contribute in a multitude of
needed ways.

Lastly, to confirm the above, all anyone needs to
do is read the Scripture and learn of how God used so
many of His key people, who in today's society would be
considered senior citizens. Many were selected by the
Lord Himself because of what they had to offer. Many of
the books of the New Testament were written by those
who enjoyed senior power. Example...

Peter, the beloved Apostle of the Lord, in his second
and last book, which by the way, was the last book to be
added to the Canon of Scripture in the New Testament;
was a book of warnings and the solemn admonition to
be diligent; to avoid false teachers, and constantly look
forward to the return of Christ. The entire book empha-
sizes Christian growth at the expense of worldly desires.
"Senior power," is achieving what Peter's life was all
about, from being a brash outspoken young man who
allowed the pressures of life, to on occasion, speak
falsehood *(his encounter with Paul when he was made
to more fully understand the truth of salvation without
the works of the law, and also the denial of Christ after
His crucifixion.)* But, Peter in my mind, could be considered one of the best examples in Scripture of the
reality of "Senior Power!" When you think of it, it's all
about growth; an ever-increasing godly attitude in following and emulating the life of Jesus Christ and His
teachings. In support of this belief, Peter was the first to
exclaim Jesus as the Son of the Living God!

When Jesus came to the region of Caesarea Philippi, he asked his disciples, "Who do people say the Son of Man is?" They replied, "Some say John the Baptist; others say Elijah; and still others, Jeremiah or one of the prophets." "But what about you?" he asked. "Who do you say I am?" Simon Peter answered, "You are the Christ, the Son of the living God." (Matthew 16:13-16)

Peter was willing to sacrifice his life, and did so by being hung on a cross, upside down... by his own choice. He understood truth. He lived it, and once he realized God's call on his life, there was no turning back. He literally "Put the Pedal to the Metal!"

This was "Senior Power" at its best. Not because of Peter's power, but because of the Power of God. And finally, to be a Senior, is not measured by the number of years you have lived, but the time of; God provided maturity, spiritual maturity.

His divine power has given us everything we need for life and godliness through our knowledge of Him who called us by His own glory and goodness. Through these He has given us His very great and precious promises, so that through them you may participate in the divine nature and escape the corruption in the world caused by evil desires. (2 Peter 1:3-4)

So, in conclusion, with the above in mind, those of you who are reading this book and have the misguided belief that quality of life may only be found in youth, have much to learn! Just remember this truth, with an open mind, one day you'll discover what I'm talking about for yourself. Think about the fact that what you believe is of utmost importance to you, and to your family. Does it meet the test of *James Chapter four? (Check it out!)* Do you relegate what YOU want as more important than what God wants for your life? How much time do you waste on the trivialities of life?

I now can look back on my life and see how I used to think about time...how it belonged to me! It was my life! Sure, I did what I thought was pleasing to God, but was it really? This is the dilemma of life. A mistaken view of the importance of walking so close to God that it's as if you can reach out and touch Him.

Maybe all of this is okay with God, but I still need to encourage each of you to pause and think about slowing down and relegating more personal time to your walk and talk with God. Never forget, as His child, He dwells within each of us, and is constantly monitoring every aspect of our lives. Why.... to help us by being our compass and personal guide in seeking the truth in all things. Senior Power can come earlier in life if you seek it!

"God's Antibiotic... the Bible"

Ever wondered why there's sin?

One of the greatest medical discoveries the world has known in recent years, is the infection fighting substance, called an "Antibiotic." Prior to its discovery, we had to depend on other medications, such as Sulfa drugs for a possible way to rid ourselves of many infectious diseases. These drugs were limited in their capability, thus the need to find something better. Now, many think we can use antibiotics for just about everything, but we've learned this is not the case. When plagued with a 'virus' of some type, the antibiotic is useless, so we just have to wait it out, and hope we will somehow survive.

In using the analogy of "God's Antibiotic" being the Bible, where it relates to spiritual matters, it's a pretty good way of thinking about it. But, like all analogies, this one isn't perfect either. Where the antibiotic fails when it comes to its fight against a virus, the Word of God, the Bible, is not plagued with the same flaw. If we view infections and viruses and their spiritual counterpart, which may be considered Sin..., for the sake of this anolgy, God has provided a once for all, cure for all, "Sin Killer," provided by Him in the form of His "one and only Son, Jesus Christ." Our belief and trust in the reality of Jesus Christ and the purpose for which He came to this planet, is an eternal "shot in the arm;" the cure for all sin we have ever, or will ever commit. A "shot in the arm" an eternal fix!

There is another part of this analogy which is exactly the same. All antibiotics, and all medications for that matter, are useless if you don't make that needed trip to see the Doctor. Most men are accused by their wives, of not doing so when it's needed! They blame the macho attitude for their extended illness, which could have been avoided. *I won't bother to list the adjectives used by these wives as they complain about the stupidity of the typical excuse they hear... but you know what I mean!*

By now you know where I'm going with this, don't you?

When it comes to your spiritual health, whether man or woman, boy or girl, you need to take a trip to see the Great Physician. The neat thing is you don't need to get in your car and go somewhere! You can stop right now as you are reading this book, and make that visit. You don't have to get on the phone, and make an appointment. And get this; you only have to make one visit! There is absolutely nothing you need to do to prepare for this visit, other than being willing, and without having any question or analysis of the methods used. The physician has the capability of eliminating your "from birth" malady called sin! Simply stated, your willingness and recognition of your lifelong sinful condition, being prompted by the Holy Spirit of God into the center of your very being, your heart, has provided all the preparation you need. Now that this preparation has been accomplished, the Great Physician can operate and provide the eternal cure we all so desperately need! It's called, "Eternal Salvation!"

Make no mistake; God, from the very beginning has focused on the spiritual health of His children. From the biblical historical perspective... in the beginning with Adam, God's first born human being, the picture becomes clear. When given the free choice to obey or disobey God, he didn't surprise God with the action he took. Unfortunately, he listened to one of God's fallen angels, Satan, which set in concrete, the future life of sin for all mankind! In reality, Adam took on the sinful form of Satan. It was by the wisdom of God, which required this choice; a choice originally given to the Angels, otherwise God would not have expelled those which rebelled, from Heaven being led by Lucifer. *(Satan)*

The scripture is clear... God cannot look upon sin! *Witness this positive proof...*

Thou art of purer eyes than to behold evil, and canst not look on iniquity: (Habakkuk 1:13) (KJV)

Also, make no mistake about the plan of God. God has always been a God of justice, both in heaven and in His entire universe, including this small speck called earth we live on. There has always been good and evil, as long as we have any knowledge of. For that, there should be no argument. What we experience in this life, and how the Bible clarifies for us this truth, we must come to the conclusion, that Scripture is abundantly clear about the past, and about the future which God holds in His hand. He alone is in control of it all, and when you think about the scripture above, and then the purpose for His sending His Son to this Earth, it now takes on new meaning and significance.

Consider the following... here's a nutshell-biblical view of our past present and future, and needs clarification usually not mentioned by biblical teachers!

Because of the love of God for His children, He sent His one and only Son, part of the Trinity of God, to be the ultimate sacrifice for our sin. The Scripture is clear when it says; "without the shedding of blood *(sacrifice)* there is no remission of sin." This was God's plan in the very beginning for His chosen people, the Jews. Then, His continuing plan to ultimately provide a once and for all sacrifice which would be available to all mankind... could only be possible by "God becoming sin for us!"

Don't miss this next point. It is paramount to our understanding of Salvation, and has generally been missing in the teaching we receive.

With the following key thought in mind... "God could not look upon sin..." He had to send His Son to become man, while still being God. The Incarnation provided the ability for the Son to 'see' sin, without having it affect His Holiness!

Therefore, now as the God-man, He could eventually die and become the sacrifice for all sin, past, present and future, for those who would accept His truth... truth as provided to us through the Word of God... not just as an historical event or record, but as a faithful promise for all who would believe regarding our eternal life with God.

[So] God, in the form of man, *(Jesus Christ)* shed His blood... willingly... as our eternal sacrifice! Again, as man He experienced the presence of sin which in turn created the ONLY opportunity for God, to become sin for us, then, when His resurrection took place, <u>I believe Jesus could not see sin any more as He did when He was the God-man</u>. Those He was in contact with after the resurrection were His followers who, in reality, were the first believer's, and as believer's were free from the condemnation of sin! The Ascension took place! Jesus left this Sin cursed world in the presence of believers who were clean of ALL sin. Now, He is at the Fathers right hand making intersession for all of His children.

His new plan took place some 2000 years ago, and the payment for sin is still available and continues for all who will believe in God... through believing and putting their trust in His Son, Jesus Christ! Simply stated it is one thing to believe there is a God, and another thing to put your trust and faith in God... through His Son, Jesus Christ.

Evil power is limited, but the power of good, as exemplified by the one and only God of the Universe, has no limit! One day in the future, all evil will be eliminated. The signposts of this future truth are becoming clearer, day by day, which we see with joy and great anticipation as we move towards God's final plan of redemption for all those who look forward to His coming.

"Redemption"

Have you ever wondered about the whole concept of redemption? We hear the word, we hear about the shedding of blood, the work of the high priest back in the days of God's laws given to the Jews... And the rituals, those laws demanded. Well, back then the people were obligated by God to keep the dietary laws and ceremonial cleansing laws which were all "External" and did nothing to completely cleanse the conscience of the worshiper, and were required on a continuing basis. Not until the coming of Jesus Christ as the Messiah, would there be a way, or method to "once and for all" cleanse and make perfectly pure, the heart and conscience of the individual. This was God's new and better way. It was called His "New Testament Covenant," or, the putting aside of the "Old Testament Covenant, so that God could enter into the individual in the form of the third person of the Godhead, the Holy Spirit. This was not true during the Old Testament period. So, no longer would there be the need for the High Priest to enter once a year into the Holy of Holies *(the inner room in the temple)* to sprinkle the blood of the choicest of goats and calves on the Ark of the Covenant. This, back then, was known as the "Day of Atonement." This annual effort by the High Priest was required to eliminate the sins of all of the Jews for one more year. *(Leviticus chapter 16)*

This ritual was required because God's people, the Jews, were "slaves to sin", and needed the inward cleansing performed by the High Priest. There was a price to pay by the people... the loss of choice goats and calves. But, the real cost was to pay the price to "buy back" a slave. Why was this? God was willing to buy back His people through their offering of animals used by the High Priest in order to cleanse them from their sin.

The beginning of the original Redemption process was when the blood of a choice animal was sprinkled on the door posts back when the Jews were slaves to the Egyptians, and God was ready to judge Pharaoh for not keeping his promise to the Jews in allowing them to leave Egypt, and be on their way to the Promised Land.

You remember the story; the firstborn of all Egyptians and Jews in Egypt would be put to death. This was God's statement to Pharaoh, but God provided "redemption" for *only* the Jewish firstborn children by this sprinkling of blood on the door posts. This isn't the complete story; we need to understand the following truth.

God's plan of salvation was instituted before the very foundation of the world. It wasn't a "reaction" caused by the expected disobedience of God's people, the Jews. No, God knew beforehand, that the Old Testament law was never to be the final answer for ultimate redemption. It was just the first step in His plan for the salvation of the entire world, not just His chosen people.

Listen to what Peter has to say about the subject...

Since you call on a Father who judges each man's work impartially, live your lives as strangers here in reverent fear. For you know that it was not with perishable things such as silver or gold that you were redeemed from the empty way of life handed down to you from your forefathers, but with the precious blood of Christ, a lamb without blemish or defect. He was chosen before the creation of the world, but was revealed in these last times for your sake. Through him you believe in God, who raised him from the dead and glorified him, and so your faith and hope are in God. (1 Peter 1:17-21)

Peter made it ultimately clear that the coming of Jesus Christ, as foretold by a host of Old Testament prophets, was the final and complete plan of Redemption. A plan for all who would hear and believe in the name of Jesus Christ as the one who has purchased their freedom from sin and the one who has provided the only way of Redemption.

"A Pair of Glasses"

By seeing with both eyes, which are brought into focus with the help of two lenses, lenses designed to provide an accurate vision of what has been illuminated by God's light, is precisely what God has provided through His Word. The Bible Testaments, both old and new, are the two lenses through which we are able to "see clearly" the complete eternal "truth" of our existing in His magnificent Universe.

Vision as opposed to blindness seems to not be the choice for most that have walked the face of this planet.

It's a paradox, when people are blind, and yet do not realize it. When told they are blind about the singular truth in existence, that of the architect and builder of the Universe, and His historical errorless document, they dismiss this information for one reason only... that of being captive to the present ruler of this World. This ruler is in charge of most people without their knowledge. They believe what we are, is the result of a Universe which just exists, a Universe with no controls other than the old mysterious "Mother Nature" which no one has any idea of how she ever came into being; nothing more than a theory of existence of some dreamer long since gone.

To say Satan's in control is "poppycock" to most. Yet, as they see the reality of sinful life, *(not a description they would use)* but the pain, sickness and death which to them are totally unavoidable... there is no answer! Thus, live life to the fullest, taking all you can take, for as long as possible, and then die. They believe it's all over then, so there's no reason to worry!

Those who see through the "Glasses" of the Word of God know better! The plan of the Maker of it all is available to all. It's our purpose in life, to introduce them to Truth. That Truth is "Jesus Christ." The God of it all!

"Spirituality, the Unseen Truth"

There is both Spiritual Light, and Spiritual Darkness. God is light. When He is removed, what remains is Spiritual Darkness, and we know that Satan is the Angel of Darkness, and all spiritual darkness is Sin!

In addition, we also know that "God is Love." With this in mind, there is a distinction which must be made. To some "Love is God." There would be no love in the world, if it were not for God. Love permeates every creature of God. Yet, many have rejected the love sacrifice

God provided through His Son Jesus. Why is this so? Those who reject God are intrinsically proud of their love for others. To them, love is their God. It is a pride focused on the ability of self love. It's a choice they make to love certain people, and effectively to hate, or disdain others. It's an expression of the ability to love things, even at the expense of people. To house idols in their heart by devoting time and energy to them, while rejecting the one who created them, and the one who has placed within them this powerful force called love. They believe "they" are love. They believe they have the choice to love who and what to love. In their minds, no one, even God has a right to tell them who and what to love.

The result: they, without even knowing it, become their own God. It is "self" over "God."

Have your children ever rejected your love for them. Have they ever told you "don't tell ME what to do!" Even though you are responsible for bringing them into the world, they have rejected you. I realize this is an imperfect analogy, but when people reject Christ it's much of the same thing.

Love is not God. *God IS love.* Love is the center of the universe. It's the purpose for which all things have been made. Today it's impossible to fully understand this truth, but when the "Day of the Lord" occurs, we will experience the totality of this word "love." We will experience "God," for he alone is love.

The New Heaven and the New Earth will become one. The opposite of love will no longer exist, not even in the memory of God, and we His children who have made the choice in this life, to believe in Him as our Savior and Lord.

This choice is still available. What will you do with your choice?

"Summation"

All of the twenty eight life challenges above, in no specific order, speak to the truth I dealt with in MSM, titled "Random" — as stated in MSM, Chapter 5, "God is in Control." *After reading the above, you may want to go back and revisit this chapter.*

My prayer, in writing MMSM, has been centered on our need to listen for the presence of the Holy Spirit as He points the way to "what's next!" As He has led, I have responded and hopefully you have realized through these relatively few subjects dealt with in this chapter, a certain pattern of life the Spirit of God is pleased with, a lifestyle conducive to creating a thirst for God in the lives of those who witness your presence as you walk with God.

God is in the business of prompting His children on an individual basis, for specific reasons only He knows. The excitement for us then, as we do our best in following His lead, is to fully enjoy the beauty of seeing the puzzle of life come together. As the picture or the puzzle is made more evident, we are privileged to realize our own expanding faith in God. The two key attributes of our Father are "Love and Justice," *(the foundation of His character)* both, while we are alive on this planet are essential. Love equals total acceptance, and justice equals right, or "complete righteousness." This, by the way, is the only thing we will have knowledge of when we will walk with Him in Heaven. The word "Justice" will no longer be needed because all "Injustice" at that time, will be non-existent.

Imagine that, no... absolutely no wrong or sinful knowledge will be part of the landscape of the New Earth and New Heaven. Nothing but pure "Agape" love, which has put to death all potential for sin, or even the very thought of it! We will experience what God promised through Jesus Christ while he was here on this Earth, when he provided this amazing statement, through the writer of Hebrews... *For I will forgive their wickedness and will remember their sins no more. (Hebrews 8:12)* Also, David penned these words... *For as high as the heavens are above the earth, so great is his love for those who fear him; as far as the east is from the west, so far has he removed our transgressions from us. As a father has compassion on his children, so the LORD has compassion on those who fear him; (Psalm 103:11-13)*

This was but a glimpse for us of having a place where sin is nonexistent and not remembered anymore. God's Word is not simply something we read or contemplate, but it is something we do. We live it, we believe it, we expose it to others, because we love the author beyond all else!

Additionally, every believer is a priest to other believers.

But you are a chosen people, a royal priesthood, a holy nation, a people belonging to God, that you may declare the praises of Him who called you out of darkness into His wonderful light. (1 Peter 2: 9)

After reading this Scripture, how can anyone who calls themselves a Christian continue to sit on their duff? Is it "conviction time" in your life?

We all can do a better job in presenting Christ to our world, and God said it wouldn't be easy. But, there is no greater joy than seeing an eternal soul, someone we love come to the saving knowledge of what Jesus Christ did for them and for all of us, so many years ago.

Remember how you got here... You once were plagued with "spiritual blindness." But something changed all that! You were made to see once again by the truths found in the Word of God.

Part 4

'Living' Accounts of Choice Servants of God

"Both Historical and Contemporary"
All in subjection to the Word of God

Followed by

The End of Life as we know It

"It's God's Judgment Time"

CHAPTER 9

MSM Filled Lives... Up

To the Brim!

Real Stories and Real People,
"Who walked the Walk, and talked the Talk
and have made Music from the Word of God."

A s I approached the development of this chapter, I felt the challenge of God to present the lives of important biblical figures, and where possible, and to present more contemporary people who mirrored, historically, the lives of those we read about in Scripture. Obviously, this is a purely subjective view on my part, and in no way is meant to indicate equality between the two. Nor, is it an effort to seek a level of comparable performance between any of the characters written about in this chapter. If anything, it's simply my desire to demonstrate, in the lives of these people, the ongoing perpetual, unchanging truth of the Word of God, regardless of the era in which they lived.

Some will be more charismatic than others. Some will demonstrate a magnificent knowledge of God's Word. Some will die an early death at the hands of those driven by the power of Satan. Some will be chosen specifically by Jesus while he was here on earth. And, no doubt all of them have been chosen by Him to bring about the perpetual, ongoing salvation of men and women, boys and girls in every corner of this world. Some will be preachers, teacher's, missionaries, and layman whose godly spirit and personal drive, has set them apart... and as David was involved in music, there will be those whose talent from God has been utilized to the fullest extent in the worship of our Savior and Lord.

In the past, someone has made the statement... less is more! So, with that thought in mind, it's my desire to keep these biographies short, sweet, and to the point. I'm sure when this chapter is complete, some will say... I wish he would've told the story of so-and-so... he or she was just fantastic! All I can say is, I've given it my best shot! Now the remaining question is: where to start?

Well, the Holy Spirit is going to have to
answer that question!

Before this decision is made...wouldn't it be great if we could go back in time and experience what the early Christians saw, felt and how they continued to exist, even after being subjected to an unbelievable litany of persecutions and even death for many who did not flinch at the demand to put aside their belief, and dedication to the Savior of the world. God's plan was underway at the behest of one powerful front runner, John the Baptist. He was there at God's command to set the stage, and open the curtain for the one whose shoestrings he was not worthy to untie! He accomplished the task. Jesus arrived on the scene at the appointed time, in order to fulfill His Father's plan of redemption.

Now, we have been privileged to enter into that scene. Our responsibility given by God, through His Son, is to take up our cross and present Jesus to those in our own personal world. This chapter is meant to put on display, men and women who have been obedient to this, their own personal task.

Join with me now, as we look through the wrong end of a telescope, and see a picture of some of God's choice servants, whose dedication to godly truth at the expense of even their lives, is an undeniable reality. Then we will expand our focus to more contemporary, godly people whose impact on individuals and the culture of their lives, is also unmistakable.

May I also say... this is the fun part in the writing of this book! It's gratifying to tell these poignant stories of "God lead, God fearing, God pleasing," individuals. People who have listened to their personal call to service, and have responded with all the fervor, strength and love for others, which God provided in advance of His specific call to each of them! There are tons and tons of more godly saints who could have graced these pages, but again, someone has said "less is more!"

Enjoy!

"Job"

After much soul-searching, as to where to start these short portraits of some of God's choicest servants... where better to start than with Job, the apparent writer of the oldest book in the Canon of Scripture. Not only is it the oldest book, but it is also the definitive work on biblical faith, its purpose and meaning, and the key reason for writing both MSM, and this sequel, MMSM.

The drama surrounding the life of Job, a prosperous and wealthy man of God, is unique in the annals of Scripture. He was the key character in this drama where God used every phase of his life, his large family, his extraordinary wealth, and of utmost importance, his knowledge and personal faith in a sovereign God. His life was a microcosm of the forces between good and evil, *(God and Satan,)* where, when we read this true account of his life, the application to our own lives is doubtless. Here, simply stated, are the key points of his life which speak in powerful terms to both heart and mind.

To make the story of faith speak loudly to all who follow Job, God allowed Satan first to destroy his wealth and his servants, and then also to kill all of his children. In spite of this horrendous destruction in his life, Job responded...

"Naked I came from my mother's womb, and naked I will depart. The Lord gave and the Lord has taken away; may the name of the Lord be praised." (Job 1:20)

Job's second test was the affliction to his body caused by Satan, and allowed by God. His wife said to him; *"Are you still holding onto your integrity? Curse God and die!" He replied, "You are talking like a foolish woman. Shall we accept good from God, and not trouble?" In all this, Job did not sin in what he said. (Job 2:9-10)*

Even his beloved wife was willing to see him sacrifice his very integrity in order to stop this satanic assault on her Husband. Of course she didn't know this was a 'God approved test on Job's life by Satan.' She believed it was his fault in trusting God, and to her this was effectively 'sinful!'

In summation, Job, after undergoing countless accusations from his wife and these so-called three friends and a young man, did not falter in his faith in God! The back and forth conversations between these four and Job, must be read in order to grasp the complete power of faith which was demonstrated in the life of Job. Finally, God rebuked these men for their legalistic attitude and comments to Job. The drama ended, and

Job was restored to happiness and wealth once again. Satan was defeated! The final result...

Faith in God was the Victor! Legalistic judgmental-ism was the loser! How some in Christendom have missed this truth, is beyond comprehension!

"Matthew"

Matthew *(Levi),* the writer of the first book of the New Testament, which was written, probably around, A.D. 60 to 70. He was a Jewish tax collector. After his call by Jesus to be one of His disciples, on the northern side of the Sea of Galilee in the city of Capernaum, he was bent on assuring all Jews of his day, that "Jesus, the Christ," was indeed the Messiah for which they had been looking for over many centuries. *Allow me to interject this reality...* Here was a man, having been selected by Jesus in spite of his checkered past, which the average Jew did not like to say the least. I imagine some could have said something like... *"How could Jesus choose a thief and a robber as one of His disciples?"* But, I'm sure it wasn't long before people like this were amazed at the change in this man's life, by virtue of just "being with Jesus!"

Well, to accomplish this task, he didn't waste any time. He began his book by providing a genealogy of Jesus Christ, as the Son of David, a genealogy going all the way back to Abraham and through King David, as the Old Testament had predicted. It is obvious when you read this book, that Matthew was a brilliant scholar of the Old Testament.

He followed this with the story of Jesus' birth and early life in the first two chapters. There was the escape to Egypt with a newborn child to avoid the edict provided by Herod to kill all the boys in Bethlehem, two years old and younger. Then after Herod died, he spoke of the return of Joseph and Mary with their brand-new Son, Jesus the Son of God... to Nazareth.

Almost 30 years had passed in the life of Jesus when Matthew, in chapter 3, begins the story of John the Baptist, his purpose in life, and ultimately the start of Jesus' ministry. What follows in the next 24 chapters of this magnificent book, is to see Jesus in action as He teaches the multitudes about His purpose in life, who He was and then to witness the dramatic events surrounding His capture and ultimate death on the cross. The book concludes with Jesus providing the Great Commission, after His resurrection, to the 11 disciples on the mountain where Jesus told them to go. When they saw Him they worshiped Him, but some doubted Him.

Allow me to provide one short example of the teachings of Christ recorded in the book of Matthew.

"Do not judge, or you too will be judged. For the same way you judge others, you will be judged, and with the measure you use, it will be measured to you. Why do you look at the speck of sawdust in your brother's eye and pay no attention to the plank in your own eye? How can you say to your brother, let me take the speck out of your eye, when all the time there is a plank in your own eye? You hypocrite, first take the plank out of your own eye, and then you will see clearly to remove the speck from your brother's eye. (Matthew 7:1-5) (Added emphasis)

Look again at that first sentence. If people would just read this, and realize they would pay the same penalty others would endure, there would be a whole lot less judging going around! *Here's what I take from this...*

The lost art of "Discernment," requires a "Consistent Persistence" in pursuing God. When we seek this ability, God says... "The door will be opened unto you," but it doesn't say, how quickly! For some people, every day is judgment day. They constantly glory in finding fault with most everything around them; people, churches, music, etc., you name it! *Does this sound familiar?* May I ask; who has the power to judge? Only God! We are to work at enlarging a discerning spirit which requires stepping back and considering all aspects of what we might otherwise judge too quickly. Usually we will find more redeeming qualities than first assumed. The admonition to be "Slow to Speak" takes on new meaning. *(James 1:19)*

This book of Matthew is crammed full of teachings directly from the mouth of our Lord Jesus Christ just like the one above. Whatever questions you may have, Jesus has an answer for all of them. The book of Matthew is a great place to start.

What better way to end this short story about one of God's chosen servants, Matthew, than to confirm the entire message of his "Book of Matthew," by quoting what Jesus had to say at the end of the last chapter after His resurrection from the dead.

Then Jesus came to them and said, "All authority in heaven and on earth has been given to me. Therefore go and make disciples of all nations, baptizing them in the name of the Father and of the Son and of the Holy Spirit, and teaching them to obey everything I have commanded you. And surely I am with you always to the very end of the age." (Matthew 28:18-20)

"John the Baptist"

In the book of Luke, Luke relates the story of the Angel of the Lord appearing to Zechariah and telling him, his wife Elizabeth who was up in years and was barren, would give birth to a son who would be called John. In addition, the Angel Gabriel made it clear to Zechariah that John would be something special. His life would be filled with the Holy Spirit from birth! This had never happened before. But Zechariah, even a man of faith, had a hard time believing he was going to be able to father a new child. Because of his disbelief, the Angel caused him to be speechless until the baby was born. After this occurred, Zechariah was no longer spoken of in Scripture. His job was accomplished, and the birth of his son John, was just as the Angel Gabriel had promised. Six months later, the same Angel Gabriel, was sent by God to Nazareth to make clear the reality of the coming of Jesus Christ to Mary and her husband Joseph. You know the rest of the story!

One additional thought...when John the Baptist was born, Zechariah's voice was returned to him. He began to speak praising God for the miracle of this birth of his new son called John. Listen to his words...

"And you, my child, will be called a prophet of the most high; for you will go on before the Lord to prepare the way for him, to give his people the knowledge of salvation through the forgiveness of their sins, because of the tender mercy of our God, by which the rising sun will come to us from heaven to shine on those living in darkness and in the shadow of death, to guide our feet into the path of peace." (Luke 1:76-79)

As is true today, it was true back then. God chose to speak through John the Baptist in a most unusual way, a man who has gone down in history as greater than any of the rulers of his day. We are guilty of judging people from a cultural point of view by what they have, not who they are. This was true of those surrounding John. In today's language he would be known as just plain weird! The clothes he wore and the food he ate, along with spending time out in the desert all by himself, placed him in a category of just being unusually different. But he was God's man. He was full of faith in God, and did exactly what God wanted him to do, and that was to preach to the people about preparing for the coming of the Lord, and to focus on "repentance" which revolved around the "law." Remember, God's grace, in the form of His Son Jesus, had not yet appeared. John could only preach about the need to follow God's commands as indicated by the law. He was harsh and hard on the people who had strayed from God. But, he also had a message for them about the coming Messiah, albeit sketchy at best, since he didn't know completely what the future message would be from Jesus.

John focused on the law, and Jesus focused on life, provided by faith and trust in Him.

John also preached about the need to be baptized in order to show your faith in God's Law and the truth of the future coming of the Messiah. He uses words like *"You brood of vipers!" Who warns you to flee from the coming wrath? Produce fruit in keeping with repentance. And do not begin to say to yourselves, "We have Abraham as our father. For I tell you that all of these stones God can raise up children for Abraham. The axe is already at the root of the trees, and every tree that does not produce good fruit will be cut down and thrown into the fire." (Luke 3:7-9)*

He mesmerized his listeners with the truth of what was happening in their lives. He did what he did out of pure faith in God and listening to God's direction for his life. Despite his unusual appearance, he caught the attention of many people. What he taught them was truthful and they listened and responded by allowing him to baptize them.

Tax collectors, soldiers, and others came and were baptized by John thinking that he might even be the Messiah, the Christ. He was a powerful man of God, but he was still just a man, a man who was sent from

God to make straight the path to Jesus Christ. In verse 21 of the same chapter, the following occurred; *when all the people were being baptized, Jesus was baptized too. "And as he was praying, heaven was opened and the Holy Spirit descended on him in bodily form like a dove." And a voice came from heaven: "You are my Son, whom I love; with you I am well pleased." (Luke 3:21-22)*

In spite of all of the above, when John was finally put in prison by Herod, he began to doubt if Jesus was the Messiah. He sought an answer to his doubt, by sending some of his disciples to ask Jesus... *"Are you the one who was to come, or should we expect someone else?" (Matthew 11:3) (Added emphasis)*

Jesus knew of John's doubtful attitude, and quickly responded...

Jesus replied, "Go back and report to John what you hear and see: The blind receive sight, the lame walk, those who have leprosy are cured, the deaf hear, the dead are raised, and the good news is preached to the poor. Blessed is the man who does not fall away on account of me."

As John's disciples were leaving, Jesus began to speak to the crowd about John: "What did you go out into the desert to see? A reed swayed by the wind? If not, what did you go out to see? A man dressed in fine clothes? No, those who wear fine clothes are in kings' palaces. Then what did you go out to see? A prophet? Yes, I tell you, and more than a prophet. This is the one about whom it is written:

"I will send my messenger ahead of you, who will prepare your way before you."

I tell you the truth: Among those born of women there has not risen anyone greater than John the Baptist;

yet he who is least in the kingdom of heaven is greater than he. From the days of John the Baptist until now, the kingdom of heaven has been forcefully advancing, and forceful men lay hold of it. For all the Prophets and the Law prophesied until John. And if you are willing to accept it, he is the Elijah who was to come. He who has ears, let him hear.
(Matthew 11:4-15)

We, who have understood and believe in the death, burial and resurrection of Jesus Christ, being the *"least in the kingdom,"* have a greater understanding and knowledge of who Jesus Christ was, than did John the Baptist, thus the statement Jesus made above, contrasting our knowledge of Jesus to that of John the Baptist.

John the Baptist' work was completed. The Savior of the world had come, and the world would never be the same.

"The Apostle John"

John and his brother James, also an Apostle of Jesus, we're both son's of Zebedee, and we're both son's of a fishing family. When "John the Baptist" arrived on the scene, it wasn't long before the Apostle John became one of his early disciples. As a disciple of John the Baptist, he was obviously tuned into the reality of Jesus Christ and the purpose for which God would send His Son into this world. Regarding his personal life, he survived his brother James by some 50 years, and died at the age of 94 to 95 years. It was James who suffered the first martyr's death of the 12 Apostles, and the Apostle John was the only one who wasn't martyred, but ultimately died on the Isle of Patmos where he was exiled. He wrote the book of John about 10 to 15 years before God took him home, in approximately A.D. 85 to 90. He authored not only the book of John, but also 1st, 2nd and 3rd John, and also, the book of Revelation.

John was a powerful writer whose purpose in life was to purposely present Jesus Christ as God himself! John makes it completely clear when Jesus was born, it wasn't His beginning. The simple statement... in the beginning WAS!

Listen to how He started this book.

In the beginning WAS the Word, and the Word WAS with God, and the Word WAS God. He WAS with God in the beginning. Through him all things were made; without him nothing WAS made that has been made. In him WAS life, and that life WAS the light of men. The light shines in the darkness, but the darkness has not understood it. (John 1:1-5)

When John states the word, "Word," he is speaking expressly of Jesus Christ. In *(Psalm 33:6)* the "Word," was an agent of creation, and was a source of God's message to His people through the prophets. When God created, He made something from nothing, including you and me! People today live without even giving any credit to their maker. They simply just... live. John's purpose was to change that attitude which I'm sure was prevalent even in his day. The writing of his book wasn't just to tell a story, but to make sure that everyone, even to this day, would understand without equivocation, that Jesus Christ was the living Son of God! He was not just another body that came along, having lived and died just like you and me. No... He was the living Son of God!

According to the Word of God, the Bible, after the disciples heard of the apparent resurrection of Jesus, John and Peter took off and ran as hard as they could to the tomb, and we know that John was the first to believe that Jesus was truly raised from the dead.

Early on the first day of the week, while it was still dark, Mary Magdalene went to the tomb and saw that the stone had been removed from the entrance. So she came running to Simon Peter and the other disciple, the one Jesus loved, and said, "They have taken the Lord out of the tomb, and we don't know where they have put him!" So Peter and the other disciple started for the tomb. Both were running, but the other disciple outran Peter and reached the tomb first. He bent over and looked in at the strips of linen lying there but did not go in. Then Simon Peter, who was behind him, arrived and went into the tomb. He saw the strips of linen lying there, as well as the burial cloth that had been around Jesus' head. The cloth was folded up by itself, separate from the linen. Finally the other disciple, who had reached the tomb first, also went inside. <u>He saw and believed</u>. (They still did not understand from Scripture that Jesus had to rise from the dead.) (John 20:1–9) (Added emphasis)

Here we see the humble spirit displayed by John when he purposely did not name himself as the one that went with Peter to the tomb, but simply referred to the other disciple as the "one Jesus loved."

Probably the greatest statement made by John in this book is recorded...

Jesus did many other miraculous signs in the presence of his disciples, which are not recorded in this book. But these are written that you may believe that Jesus is the Christ, the son of God, and that by believing you may have life in his name. (John 20:30-31)

But arguably, the most important Scripture in the entire Bible, and the most well known is:

For God so loved the world that he gave his one and only son, that whosoever believes in him shall not perish but have eternal life. (John 3:16)
(Added emphasis)

When Jesus selected John, He knew precisely what he would accomplish on His behalf, and how the words which he wrote, would prepare multiple thousands of people across this globe for their eternal life relationship with God. The Lord allowed John to live a long life in order to accomplish the task which was set before him. When we look at his life, he was special to God, but I believe, we who have named the name of Christ in our hearts and lives, are just as special.

"The Apostle Peter"

Matthew, in chapter 4 of his book, provides us with the historical reality of how Jesus began to seek out and to command His future disciples to follow Him. The first two were Simon Peter and his brother Andrew. The Scripture tells us they were in the process of casting their nets in order to make a living as fishermen. *"Come, follow me," Jesus said, "and I will make you fishers of men." At once they left their nets and followed him. (Matthew 20:19-20)*

1st and 2nd Peter we're written, quite possibly from Rome around A.D. 62 to 67. Peter wrote his first book as an encouragement to all the suffering Christians at that time. This was when the Great Persecution under Emperor Nero began. Throughout the whole Roman Empire, Christians were being tortured and killed for their faith. In addition, the church in Jerusalem was being scattered throughout the Mediterranean world. Peter knew what it was like to be persecuted for his faith. He had seen many fellow Christians face death at the hands of the Romans.

They were tortured and many killed for the cause of Christ.

He opens his first book by thanking God for salvation, giving us the example we should follow, and how trials aren't necessarily bad, but are God's way for us to exercise our faith. He taught they should continue to believe in Him, regardless of their circumstances. To live holy lives with a reverent spirit towards God and trust in Him, and to make sure they live their lives honestly as they seek to become more like Christ. *The following is a "must" read...*

Praise be to the God and Father of our Lord Jesus Christ! In his great mercy he has given us new birth into a living hope through the resurrection of Jesus Christ from the dead, and into an inheritance that can never perish, spoil or fade—kept in heaven for you, <u>who through faith are shielded by God's power until the coming of the salvation that is ready to be revealed in the last time</u>. In this you greatly rejoice, though now for a little while you may have had to suffer grief in all kinds of trials. These have come so that your faith—of greater worth than gold, which perishes even though refined by fire—may be proved genuine and may result in praise, glory and honor when Jesus Christ is revealed. Though you have not seen him, you love him; and even though you do not see him now, you believe in him and are filled with an inexpressible and glorious joy, for you are receiving the goal of your faith, the salvation of your souls. (1 Peter 1:3-9) (Added emphasis)

These succinct powerful words delivered by the apostle Peter, summarizes the meaning and purpose of faith. Peter penned these words while in Rome, during the period when Emperor Nero began the "Great

Persecution" of the church. The church in Jerusalem was in the process of being scattered, and Peter, who eventually would be executed, wrote to all those who were experiencing this persecution for their living faith in Jesus Christ.

As you read this amazing book, you'll see firsthand, the hand of God at work. Here was a man chosen by God to be used to propagate the Gospel of Christ, and who was given his name by Jesus Christ, which means "Rock." Peter used this conception of the church, a "Spiritual House" built on the foundation of Christ as the Chief Cornerstone and a spiritual house composed of living stones built upon Christ.

In the second chapter, he challenges them to rid themselves of all kinds of malice and deceit, hypocrisy envy, and slander of every kind. Then, to seek the opposite which was a craving for the pure spiritual milk of God's Word. After this, he teaches about the living stone and a chosen people. Listen to these powerful words in

As you come to Him, the living stone–rejected by men but chosen by God and precious to Him–you also, like living stones, are being built into a spiritual house to be a holy priesthood, offering spiritual sacrifices acceptable to God through Jesus Christ. For in Scripture it says: "See, I lay a stone in Zion, a chosen and precious <u>cornerstone</u>, and the one who trusts in Him (<u>the cornerstone</u>) will never be put to shame." (1 Peter 2:4-6) (Added emphasis)

Again, the cornerstone Peter is speaking about is none other than Jesus Christ. There are those in Christendom who misinterpret Scripture as it applies to the Apostle Peter. They mis-apply the meaning of *(Matthew 16:17-19)* where Jesus is speaking to Peter and calls him a stone, or a rock. Peter was just that, he was a rock but he was not the cornerstone. Listen to the above Scripture...

Jesus replied, "Blessed are you, Simon son of Jonah, for this was not revealed to you by man, but by my Father in heaven. And I tell you that you are Peter, and on this rock I will build my church, and the gates of Hades will not overcome it. I will give you the keys of the kingdom of heaven; whatever you bind on earth will be bound in heaven, and whatever you loose on earth will be loosed in heaven."

This was Jesus' answer to Peter after Peter had answered Jesus' question, namely *"Who do you say I am?" Simon Peter answered, "You are the Christ, the Son of the living God." (Matthew 16:15-16)* Therefore, since Peter was the first to identify Jesus as the Messiah, he was then given the power to become the leader of the church of Jesus Christ, the first great leader in the church at Jerusalem. It wasn't any local church or a church that gained its power from the state, but the first effective church for Jesus Christ in Jerusalem. This came about because it was the teaching from Peter that identified Jesus as the Chief Cornerstone, or the Rock. Peter was a rock but he was not the cornerstone as Jesus has so clearly identified. To make Peter anything but what Jesus made him, is heresy and is to do disservice to the clear contextual understanding of Scripture.

These two significant books in the Bible, which were the "cement" of the church structure, propelled the Christian church through and past this time of persecution and effort made to silence Christianity. The basic themes of his two letters were... Salvation... Persecution... God's family... Family life... Judgment... False teachers, and finally Christ' return. When read with an open mind and heart, it's impossible not to see and understand why Jesus selected this most unusual individual, to carry the living torch of God's New Testament plan of redemption for the human race.

From a personality point of view, Peter was a "take charge sort of person." Later in life, he was to experience a softening of his typical bombastic sort of approach to everything. There was demonstrable change in his life because of the teachings he received from Jesus. He's a wonderful example of what can happen in a person's life when they submit themselves to Jesus Christ, through the Bible, His personal Word to each one of us.

"The Apostle Paul"

The apostle Paul was born around the same time as Christ. His given name was Saul, and grew up in the city of Tarsus which was a University town, a town which provided him with an unusually good education. Saul's father was of the tribe of Benjamin, so he was Jewish through and through. In the book of Acts, he defended who he was.

"Then Paul, knowing that some of them were Sadducees and the other's Pharisees, called out in the Sanhedrin, "My brothers, I am a Pharisee, the son of a Pharisee. I stand on trial because of my hope in the Resurrection of the dead." (Acts 23:6)

He also made it clear as to his background in Philippians.

Circumcised on the eighth day, of the people of Israel, of the tribe of Benjamin, a Hebrew of Hebrews; in regard to the law, a Pharisee; as for zeal, persecuting the church; as for legalistic righteousness, faultless. (Philippians 3:5-6)

Here was a very bright young man with all the credentials necessary to be used of God as the "Missionary of all Missionaries." However, it wasn't until after Christ ministry, death and resurrection, that Saul came on the scene as one who was sent out to stop Christianity in its tracks, by persecuting and killing its converts. Those put to death included Stephen, who became the church's first martyr. It is recorded that Saul never came face-to-face with Jesus prior to His resurrection, but one day on the road to Damascus, a trip designed to continue his opposition to Christianity, he was confronted in person by Jesus Christ *(Acts 9:1-9) including Christ's statement: "Saul, Saul, why do you persecute me?"* When Saul got up from the ground, he realized he was blind. The men traveling with him and took him to Damascus, where Ananias, who was directed by the Lord, went to see Saul and placed his hands on him, restoring his sight. He immediately got up and was baptized by Ananias. His life was changed forever!

He later became an Apostle of Jesus Christ because of this event in his life, and went on to become what Jesus had planned for him. He made three long missionary journeys preaching the Gospel of Jesus Christ, while starting new churches all throughout the Roman Empire. Having spent much time in Roman jails, he authored the following books of the New Testament.

They are: Romans, 1 & 2 Corinthians, Galatians, Ephesians, Philippians, Colossians, 1 & 2 Thessalonians, 1 & 2 Timothy, Titus, and Philemon.

His life is a demonstration of the power of God to change a person's heart, typically a heart full of pride, driven by sin and the power of Satan. That day on the road to Damascus, Saul, who later had his name changed to Paul by the Lord, experienced a direct confrontation with God. All humanity has the opportunity to experience that same direct call from God as did Paul. But now, that call is provided by the Holy Spirit, the third person of the Trinity. If, and when you experience this same call... Accept it, without hesitation just as Saul of Tarsus did!

"James, *the brother of Jesus*"

I n conclusion of this, the 7th biography, of key biblical personages who have affected, and infected people the world over for the cause of Christ, what better person to discuss than James, the brother of Jesus, whose key focus in this short letter, which some have said could be considered a "how-to book on Christian living," was the subject of Godly faith. James instinctively knew there would be those who would challenge the whole concept of faith, at least from the New Testament perspective. He wrote this book primarily to the first century Jewish Christians who lived in Gentile communities, people who were persecuted Christians and who were once part of the Jerusalem church. As one of the Key Pillars of the Jerusalem church, little is known about this man except for various small references by Paul and Peter.

When you read the book of James, you will soon learn that he doesn't mince any words! He is direct and to the point. He takes to task, those who talk the talk, but don't walk the talk. You know... those people which today have been called "Nominal Christians." If James were alive today, I'm sure he would not use that designation, since there can be no Christian, which is not a real Christian. To call yourself Christian simply as a designation of sorts, is to do injustice to those early people who were called Christians because of their fervor and belief in whom Jesus Christ was, and who lived by His teachings. The book of James therefore, was written to draw a black and white distinction around the process of living for Christ. *Example...*

Consider it pure joy, my brothers, whenever you face trials of many kinds, because you know that the testing of your faith develops perseverance. Perseverance must finish its work so that you may be mature and complete, not lacking anything. If any of you lacks wisdom, he should ask God, who gives generously to all without finding fault, and it will be given to him. But when he asks, he must believe and not doubt, because he who doubts is like a wave of the sea, blown and tossed by the wind. That man should not think he will receive anything from the Lord; he is a double minded man, unstable in all he does.
(James 1:1-8)

There is no room for Nominal thinking Christians in this biblical passage! Then, allow me to conclude this short biography, with James' powerful statement on faith and works.

What good is it, my brothers, if a man claims to have faith but has no deeds? Can such faith save him? Suppose a brother or sister is without clothes and daily food. If one of you says to him, "Go, I wish you well; keep warm and well fed," but does nothing about his physical needs, what good is it? In the same way, faith by itself, if it is not accompanied by action, is dead. But someone will say, "You have faith; I have deeds." Show me your faith without deeds, and I will show you my faith by what I do. (James 2:14-18)

Consider this short analogy... If a man says he's a carpenter and when asked to prove, or demonstrate his ability as a carpenter, and is not able to pound one nail into a board, would you call him a "Nominal Carpenter?" I don't believe so! The truth of the matter is the church needs to come to grips, on an individual, person by person basis, with what EACH ONE IS before the Lord.

You're either a Christian, in the true sense and meaning of the word, or you're not! There is no in-between!

James came to grips with this reality, because in the early life of his brother Jesus, some in the family did not want to believe he was who He said he was! We don't know if James was included as one of those doubters, but the powerful teaching of Jesus and His direction provided to James, His brother, resulted in this fantastic Epistle, a book worth memorizing, and a book which challenges all of us to "Walk the Walk, and Talk the Talk!

The following short biographies are about more contemporary people who were, and are all sold out to the Lord. Each one has taken heart with the teaching of James which we've just discussed. Some have gone on to be with the Lord, and some are still alive, serving Him with every ounce of strength they can muster. Everyone, a true born-again believer in Jesus Christ; in fact, every Christian could have their biography in this book if it were possible... Because we are all the same in Jesus! There are no 'teacher's pets' with Him. That was true of the seven wonderful people we have just read about, and the six who follow who have named the name of Jesus as their only Lord and Savior. "To God be the glory!" Amen!

"Harold Ray Henniger"[2]

It was the summer of 1968, I believe, when our family decided on a vacation trip to Gatlinburg Kentucky. We decided that first evening, after arriving at our motel, to have dinner on the north end of town, at a long since departed, log cabin style restaurant. After being seated at the back of the restaurant, overlooking a fast-moving creek, *(a wonderful memory I might add,)* we soon had our food delivered to the table. During that time, a man and his wife and two children entered the restaurant, and were seated close to the front. For some reason, this man caught my attention. I said to Gale, "I believe I've seen this man somewhere before? He looks like a preacher to me!"

We finished our dinner, and on the way out I felt compelled to stop and talk to him. I said something straightforward like... "Excuse me, but are you a Baptist preacher?" He quickly smiled, and said; "Yes I am, I'm Harold Henniger from Canton Baptist Temple in Canton Ohio, this is Carmine my wife, and John and Joy." The conversation was relatively short, we told them who we were... where we were from, and thanked them for the short conversation.

Almost 10 years later, on December 30, 1977, we joined Canton Baptist Temple after moving from Toledo to start a new operation for the company I worked for. Believe it or not, when we joined the church, the moment Pastor Harold saw us, he was quick to remark... "You're Bob and Gale Park from Toledo Ohio, what brings you to Canton?

That was Harold Henniger! He was a magnificent people person! I believe he knew everyone in the church by their first name. *(I sometimes wonder if he made that part of this life, just like Charles Haddon Spurgeon had done?)*

He tells this short story about the birth of the "Christian Hall of Fame,"[2] a dream which came true in his lifetime.

"The Christian Hall of Fame was born in my mind as I lay in Aultman Hospital, recovering from a heart attack which I experienced in November, of 1964. After reading the 11th chapter of Hebrews, I heard a radio announcement referring to the Professional Football Hall of Fame, which is located in our city. The idea came to me that we should put "God's Heroes" on display at our church: the

men, who through the centuries have stood for the faith once and for all delivered to the saints.

The main purpose of the Christian Hall of Fame is inspirational, not merely educational. It is our prayer that as a result of viewing the likenesses of these men and women, and reading their biographies, many will be inspired to carry the bloodstained banner of the cross around the world as missionaries; that men will be called into the ministry to preach the unsearchable riches of Christ; and that all be led to a life dedicated to the honor of Him who loved us and washed us from our sins in His own blood, even our Lord Jesus Christ. To him be the glory." The following biography is part of the Christian Hall of Fame[2] in Canton Ohio.

Harold Ray Henniger 1924 – 2004

Harold Henniger was born May 4, 1924, in Doylestown, Ohio. At the age of 15, he was saved at the Akron Baptist Temple, where Dallas Billington pastored, and became his mentor. After his conversion, he led the youth department, where he met his future wife, Carmine Sims, who was the pianist for the group. Together, they have three children; Jim, John and Joy.

After serving on a hospital ship in the US Army during World War II, he graduated from Baptist Bible Seminary of Fort Worth Texas. While in seminary he was an assistant to Dr. J Frank Norris, at the First Baptist Church, and served as superintendent of the Junior Department, young people's class, and faithfully taught an adult class of 500.

Henninger accepted the pastorate at Canton Baptist Temple in 1947, and began his pastorate serving over 40 years. When he accepted the call, the church attendance, including two babies in the nursery, was 143. By the fall of 1971 the attendance was over 5200.

He received an Honorary Doctorate from Bob Jones University, served as president of Baptist Bible Fellowship International, led the church in building two edifices, and led a staff of eight ministers along with eight secretaries. Henniger had a vision for reaching Canton Ohio for Christ. Upon his arrival in Canton, he began a radio broadcast with both morning and evening services "live" over a local station, and later began a television ministry which also aired a "live" service. He became well-known and well-liked in the city. He was one of the original inductees to the Stark County Wall of Fame housed at the McKinley Museum.

In 1964 as he lay in the hospital after experiencing a heart attack, God laid upon his heart to organize a Christian Hall of Fame. The hall is located at Canton Baptist Temple and currently includes 103 original oil portraits of men and women who have influenced the history of Christianity through the centuries. In 1969 under his leadership, the church purchased a youth camp *(naming it Camp CHOF after the Christian Hall of Fame)* where over 1200 young people attended each summer, ending with a family Bible conference.

His pastorate spanned some 43 years, and at the age of 65 he became Pastor Emeritus. After retiring, he taught the ambassador Sunday school class where over 250 met each Sunday morning. This class included several members who started with him in 1947. He taught his last lesson September 5, 2004. On October 25, 2004, Dr. Harold Henniger met face-to-face, the Lord and Savior he had so faithfully served.

"George Beauchamp Vick"[2]

Everyone knew this man simply by "Dr. Vick." He was our pastor for many years prior to our move to Chicago. Temple Baptist Church in Detroit Michigan was one of the largest churches in the nation at that point in time. The Page family, Gale's mom and dad and sister, had been members there ever since their arrival from Kentucky many years earlier. If you've read MSM, you know something about this wonderful church, its growth under the leadership of Dr. Vick, and a power-house for the salvation of many souls.

When Gale's mom and dad celebrated their 25th wedding anniversary at a party we prepared for them at our home in Taylor Michigan, Dr. Vick and his wife Eloise were there. As the baritone in the Temple Tones quartet, which included Jimmy Vick, the first tenor, we sang a few songs on that occasion. Dr. Vick also had a great sense of humor, and wouldn't have been any-where else that evening because of his love and appre-ciation for my wonderful Father-in- law, Paul Page, and Mary his wife.

In 1975, while living in Toledo, Ohio, the news of the passing of Dr. Vick, while in his office at Baptist Bible College in Springfield Missouri came to us. It was a time of intensive grief for everyone involved in his life. He was a man of many talents, but never really felt that he was called to be a preacher. And I'll never forget his funeral in Detroit. It lasted well over four hours, with many Eulogies given by pastors from all over the country. Prior to his death, while we were living in Toledo, we had the opportunity to invite him to our church for a series of meetings. Every night after each meeting, we had the opportunity of being with him to enjoy some food together, and to listen to his many enjoyable sto-ries. He was a wonderful brother in Christ! The fol-lowing biography is part of the Christian Hall of Fame[2] in Canton Ohio.

George Beauchamp Vick 1901 – 1975

George Beauchamp Vick was born in Russellville, Kentucky, the son of a lawyer politician. When young Beauchamp was a year old, his father quit politics and entered Louisville seminary, as a student pastor. As a young child, Vick assisted his ailing father on pastoral visits, and the experience undoubtedly influenced his later emphasis on the visitation program as the key to church growth.

Vicks first paid position was the superintendence of the young People's Department at J Frank Norris's First Baptist Church in Fort Worth Texas. Under Vicks dynamic leadership, the department averaged nearly 1000 per Sunday, and annually led First Baptist in additions.

In 1929 Vick "hit the sawdust trail" as the advance man – song leader for evangelist Wade House and Mordecai Ham. In 1936, Ham had a revival at the Temple Baptist Church in Detroit where Norris was attempting a dual pastorate. Due to the 1300 mile distance involved, Norris was unable to conserve the results achieved during his visits; thus Vick was induced to assume the role of general superintendent, which due to Norris' protracted absences, was tantamount to the Pastorate. He became co-pastor in 1948 and soul pastor in 1950.

For nearly 40 years overall Vick led the Temple Baptist Church to the pinnacle of influence among fundamentalists. During that period, he also became president of the World Fundamentalist Baptist Missionary Fellowship, president of the Bible Baptist Seminary, president of Baptist Bible College, primary founder and titular head of the Baptist Bible Fellowship, leading figure in the Fundamentalist Baptist Congress, and the spiritual diplomat who most successfully bridged the gaps between the various fundamentalist islands.

"Fanny Crosby"[2]

Francis Jane Crosby 1820 – 1915

Jane Crosby was born in southeast New York. When she was six weeks old she lost her sight through the negligence of the attending physician. At the age of nine her grandmother introduced Fannie to the Bible which he began to devour.

She learned to repeat from memory the Pentateuch, the book of Ruth, many of the Psalms, the book of Proverbs, Song of Solomon and much of the New Testament.

Near her 15th birthday, she was enrolled in the Institute for the blind in New York City, and spent the next 23 years there as a student and teacher.

From her earliest childhood, she felt the urge to write poetry. While at the Institute, her poems attracted the attention of many famous people, and in 1843 at the age of 23, she was a guest of Congress. She paid tribute to the Congress within the original home, and then began paying tribute to the Lord, reciting verses about the tender care of a loving Savior. With all of her apparent devotion to Christ, she was really not converted until 1851 during a revival. Soon her poems began to reflect her faith in Christ and from her prolific pen came the words of such songs as... "A shelter in the time of storm," "All the way my Savior leads me," "Blessed assurance," "Close to thee," "He hideth my soul," "I am thine old Lord," "Jesus is calling," "My Savior first of all," "Near the cross," "Safe in the arms of Jesus," "Tell me the story of Jesus," "To God be the glory," and nearly 9000 others.

Though blind, she lived to see 100 million copies of her songs printed. After a full life of devotion to her Savior, she slipped away to meet Him and to see Him face-to-face, just short of her 95th birthday. On her

gravestone in Bridgeport Connecticut, are the words...
"She hath done what she could."

"Jerry Falwell"²

J erry Falwell just liked to be called Jerry, at least
that's what he told me when we visited one Christmas
season when they had their annual Christmas program, which included a huge Christmas tree filled with
people! It wasn't the first time we were there, because
our youngest daughter Sandy attended the college,
and while there, became part of the nationally known
singing group called, "The Sounds of Liberty." Note, in
MSM, you can read the complete story about this wonderful daughter of ours and her association with both
the school and Jerry Falwell. She has a great picture of
Jerry hugging her which she cherishes to this day.

On the personal side, Jerry and I have at least one
thing in common, and that's the year of our birth, but
that's where it ends!

By the time we reached Toledo, the Old Time Gospel
Hour was a weekly staple in our spiritual diet at the
Park household. We just loved this man's tenacity for
making clear the Scriptures concerning everyone's
need of Jesus Christ in their life. When it came time
for Sandy to head off to college, there was no question
where it would be. Back then, it was Liberty Baptist
College. Jerry's message was a powerful rendering of
the "Grace of God." There was no room in his teaching
for some of the pharisaical tendencies others in the fundamentalist movement seemed to have had. He was all
about the teachings of Paul and his demand for people
to understand the Grace of God, without the pressure
of applying manmade rules for life and acceptance by
the church. In that regard, he was a bit of a renegade,

from these who propagated the so called, "fundamentalist circles."

The Christian Hall of Fame biography below, paints a vivid picture of this God directed, "Man of God."

Jerry Lamon Falwell 1933 – 2007

Jerry Falwell was born in Lynchburg, Virginia, the son of an agnostic local businessman/bootlegger and a Christian mother. When he was a boy with little interest in the church, his mother would tune into Charles E. Fuller's Old-Fashioned Revival Hour, while Jerry and his twin brother Gene were in bed, so they would hear the gospel. It was not until he was a college journalism student at Lynchburg College, that Jerry realized his need for the Savior. At age 18 he accepted Jesus Christ as his Lord and Savior. From that time on, he was committed to reaching people with the gospel.

His first endeavor in ministry was remarkable, taking over a Sunday school class for boys while a student at Baptist Bible College in Springfield, Missouri. On the first Sunday, one boy attended. It was then that the Falwell's bulldog spirit began to show. He printed up invitations and handed them out to boys throughout the city, inviting them to his class. Soon, dozens of boys were attending and learning about Jesus. That same tenacity arrived with Falwell when he returned to his hometown under God's calling, to start a church. On the first Sunday, June 17, 1956, Thomas Road Baptist Church welcomed 35 people. Falwell committed to visiting every home in Lynchburg, often working well into the night to invite people to the new church in the former Donald Duck Bottling Plant. On the church's first anniversary, more than 1000 attended Sunday services. By 1969 average attendance had passed the 2000 level. The church continued rapid growth throughout the years, eventually counting more than 20,000 members. Falwell was also able to see his father come to know Christ.

Falwell also became a pioneer in Christian broadcasting, beginning with a local radio broadcast, and ultimately creating the old Time Gospel Hour Telecast which was eventually relayed on 390 television stations in America and abroad. It was through his nationally televised church service, that Falwell began to tell young people about a new college that was starting in Lynchburg. In the school's initial year of 1971, a handful of pioneering students enrolled at Lynchburg Baptist College. But again, rapid growth took place in the coming years. Today, Liberty University is the largest and most influential Christian college in America. The school is a continuation of Falwell's stated heartbeat of training young people to serve Christ.

Falwell, is also remembered for his efforts to call America back to its Judeo-Christian roots through the "Moral Majority," which was launched in 1979. It was through this endeavor that religious conservatives were awakened to become a driving force in the 1980 election of Ronald Reagan as our nation's 40th president. Falwell remained a cultural warrior throughout his life. Under the auspices Of Thomas Road Baptist Church, many nationally recognized ministries were launched under his guidance, including: Liberty Christian Academy; DEL house for alcoholic and drug addicted men; The Liberty God Parent home for unwed mothers; the Family Life Services adoption agencies; the Center for Global Missions; and many others.

Throughout his ministry, Dr. Falwell was also an unwavering friend of Israel, urging Christians to never forget the Biblical mandate to pray for the peace of Jerusalem. Following his passing in 2007, his son Jerry Junior took the reins of leadership of Liberty University as Chancellor. His son Jonathan followed in his father's footsteps as pastor Of Thomas Road Baptist Church.

Daughter Jeannie is a renowned surgeon in Virginia. Falwell was married to Macel for 49 years and was the proud grandfather of eight who knew him as "Poppy."

"Wally Stuchul"[3]

Here's a man I've had the personal opportunity to watch from the sidelines, for most of the 33+ years we've lived in the Canton Ohio area. In many ways, he replicates my hero, my father, Verne Hugh Park. You'll soon see why I've chosen to include him in this short list of people who've "Walked the Walk and Talked the Talk.

His life speaks loudly about the reality that Jesus is no "Respecter of Persons." God does not look upon worldly accomplishment or even academic spiritual accomplishment in a greater way than just the common man. His focus is on the believer's heart, regardless of position in life. My friend Wally is an amazing example of Christ's expectation for all of us.

Ralph Wallace Stuchul 1922 - Now in his 89th year.

It was some 56 years ago, in October of 1955, when Wally's heart was changed, when he came face-to-face with the need to make a choice between a life of sin, or a life of walking with Jesus Christ. He excitedly chose the latter! Interestingly enough, he was 33 years old!... Hmmm!

Like my father, Wally worked in the shop of a man-ufacturing facility called Republic Steel. If something needed fixing, he was the guy they came to. His job was necessary in order to earn a living, but his heart's desire was somewhere else! With his newfound faith in the Lord, he was quickly thrust into service by one of the superintendents of the children's department at Canton

Baptist Temple. As he shared this with me, he said something like; *"You want me to be a teacher, when I know hardly anything about the Bible?"* The superintendent replied, *"I'll give you all you need to teach a lesson every Sunday morning. This way, you'll learn right along with what the kids learn."* He taught these kids for some seven years.

Wally took that experience, and amplified it by leading these boys in the game of basketball. He organized 6 teams with 10 boys each, and each team had their own coach. He was like a father to them, and made sure that even in playing basketball you played the game like a Christian should play the game.

In 1982, Wally retired from Republic steel. Now he could devote his time and energies into serving the Lord in a most unique way! He loved working down at the church bus garage. As work was accomplished by the mechanics, he began to gather up all the scrap involved in this work, and take it to a scrap dealer. The money he earned by doing this, was used in the purchase of tools for the bus garage. He did this for some time, until the Lord touched his heart, and gave him a new motivation.

Wally loved Camp CHOF, the church's summer camp for children located about 20 miles to the west of Canton Ohio. The name 'Camp CHOF' was derived from the "Christian Hall of Fame," which Pastor Harold Henniger had already established.

Where there were kids present... you would find Wally, and after he decided to give up his teaching position, he became involved with the High School young people's class, simply as a mentor, and someone they could go to when needed.

Example; when we had "Park Place" in the basement of our home, and would have the young people over for the evening, Wally would be there "doing his thing." The kids loved him, and still do!

But, now back to his "New Found Motivation." When you have a heart and mind like Wally, you'll find ways to use your talents for God. *(That should be a lesson to all of us)* Wally learned that he could make money by collecting junk metal and selling it. So, what better way to help the hundreds of young people in the city of Canton that didn't have enough money to go to camp every year! The cost for camp this year... $165/child.

This year, 2011, there were 117 kids that didn't have the money to go. Some of them were financed by an offering which was received in Sunday school, but the majority came from scrap, lying all around our city, which an 89-year-old Wally Stuchul would pile into up his pickup truck every day, and take to the scrap dealer!

To top it all off, at the end of the camping season, Wally paid for ice cream for everyone at the Sweet Shop, adults included!

Is an entrepreneur/junk dealer welcome in Heaven? You bet!

Every Sunday when we come to church, and we see Wally, he never fails to ask... "How are the girls doing?" The girls he's speaking of, now all have grown children. But he still cares about them! *That's Wally Stuchul!*

Wally was married to Juanita, who went home to be with the Lord in the year 2000. God blessed them with two boys... Rodney Dean *(Rod)* and Wallace Lynn *(Wally)*

"Verne Hugh Park"

This was my hero, my father, as you may know from reading MSM. He was born January 1, 1905 in Plympton Township, Canada *(a New Year's Day baby... what a way to bring in the New Year)*

His accomplishments for the Lord in his lifetime, from my perspective, could easily put him in the same category as a man chosen by Jesus to be one His disciples. He wasn't a special somebody, but was special to God! When, and if, you read MSM, I believe you will understand these prejudicial thoughts of mine, and realize here was a man, who, when he appears in the Kingdom of God, will be surrounded by a host of people who arrived on the scene, because of his "never give up attitude" and desire to see men and women, boys and girls learn the truth of God's salvation through Jesus Christ His Son.

He made his journey to Heaven three months after my wonderful mother made hers. It was July 26, 1985 when I stood next to his bed side holding his hand, when his Lord and Master reached down and extracted his spirit, leaving behind a tired and worn-out body, which one day will escape the grave when Jesus gives the command.

The following short story of his life is nothing but a miniaturized portrait of what you'll find in MSM... Enjoy!

When dad reached the ripe old age of 18 years he went to his dad and mom and said,

"I believe God is leading me to go to Yankee Land."

But I never learned what the reaction to this news was from the two of them. My best guess is grandma wasn't too pleased, but grandpa, being the entrepreneur of the family, was probably more proud than anyone will ever know. The die was set. The decision was made. *"I'm headed for America."*

Before leaving on a bus to Detroit Michigan, grandpa spent some time with dad cautioning him on all the different kinds of problems he would most likely face in the big city of Detroit. He helped him plan for this day, and even gave him a money belt, which he was instructed to wear right next to his skin. The pouch in the belt to "house the money," was to be right in the middle of his back. Apparently grandpa insisted he carry all of his money with him, and not to be too quick to put it in a bank. I guess banks back then were not to be trusted, at least in grandpa's mind.

Dad complied... worked to get everything in order, and at the appointed time was on his way to Detroit Michigan, USA. The year 1923 was fast approaching! I've tried to think about his mindset during this period in his life, and I believe his decision was prompted by what his older brother Lawrence had already gone through years before. "If he can do it, I can do it," could well have been part of his motivation.

It was now 1923, the economy was fairly good and it didn't take him long to find work. He worked at several different jobs until he found one he seemed to enjoy, as a steel worker, not the best choice, but it would do. I remember him telling me about working high up in the steel structures of new large buildings in downtown Detroit. He wasn't afraid of heights! He talked about being able to catch red-hot rivets as they were thrown up to him while connecting the huge beams together. Oh, how proud I was of him as he told me so many stories.

One in particular was about a large Catholic church on Woodward Avenue, and dad was part of the group picked to install a gold statue of Mary, the mother of Jesus, atop the church steeple. He said they literally put a rope around her neck to raise her to the top of the steeple. This method caused a ruckus with the people of the church and must've been something to witness!

Well, back to the money belt. It wasn't long after he arrived in Detroit, and while returning home from work on a crowded streetcar, something occurred which he didn't discover until he got home. It was winter, and as he took off his long overcoat, he discovered a scary reality! Someone had cut a big hole in the back of his coat! He couldn't believe it! What was this all about? THEN he realized what had happened. He quickly dropped his pants and unbuckled the money belt... *and*, the worst fear, which he could have had, was realized.

All Of His Money Was Gone!

In the crowded streetcar, someone who most likely had seen him in the bathroom, and saw his money belt, was able to accomplish what seemed to be an unbelievable and impossible feat... dad was devastated! I don't know the details of what happened afterwards, but I'm sure grandpa Park came to his aid since the belt was his idea.

Again, the complete story of dad's life, and how God used him in many miraculous ways in the salvation of hundreds of people, is told in detail, in MSM.

In conclusion;

These short stories of 13 wonderful servants of God, serve to project the reality of the power of the God we serve, and His ability to influence many thousands of people over these last 2000 years of recorded history, people who have come to the knowledge of God's salvation through the preaching and teaching of His Word, the Bible. Have you joined his Army? It's never too late, as long as you're still alive.

CHAPTER 10

When Time is no More!

"Life as we know it ceases to be"

"The Judgment Seat of Christ"

There are those, who through the simplicity of their understanding of Scripture, have mistakenly come to believe what the purpose of God is, and what His actions are, in the coming judgment called *"The Judgment Seat of Christ,"* which will occur after the Rapture of the Church. This judgment is only for "Born again Believers." A wonderful time each believer in Jesus Christ to look forward to! *(The "Great White Throne" judgment is for all unbelievers. This will occur later.)*

Ironically, this judgment, in the minds of some, is this: *"For our Lord to make known, through our life testimony, in His presence, both good and bad to all whom are present, each and every believer, including those actions of life which were pleasing to God and then, any un-confessed sin prior to our death before seeing Jesus face-to-face."*

This seems to be an attempt to create guilt for sin, and for the Christian to state the need for confession for all sin prior to death. Otherwise, we will be *"ashamed and saddened"* at having those un-confessed sins brought to light in front of all present, by our Savior and Lord Jesus Christ. God certainly expects His children to pray to Him acknowledging our sin and as we communicate with Him on a continuing basis, not because we need for Him to forgive once again, but just for us to once again, acknowledge what we know is wrong in our life. Confession is always good for the soul! But let me be clear, this has nothing to do with this coming Judgment.

This teaching is in direct opposition of Jesus' teaching that all of our sin, past, present and future is removed at the moment of salvation, "as far as the East is from the West." Therefore this judgment is not about our Salvation and any un-confessed sin prior to death, but about our work for the Lord. We will not be able to testify about our sin, because it is gone! And, God has promised to *"Remember them no more!"*

Allow me to explain this mistaken view, but before doing so, *listen to the following Scripture.*

For we must all appear before the judgment seat of Christ, that each one may receive what is due him for the things done while in the body, whether good or bad. (2 Corinthians 5:10)

Based on this scripture, which begs this question: What do we receive for the so called "Bad" things? Will the Christian be punished in some way at this judgment? Answer: We will receive loss for what we could have earned, because of our lack of effort and concern for the things of God. There is nothing in scripture which, either directly, or indirectly suggests we will be reprimanded for the things we could have accomplished, but failed to do. No, *only this...we will simply receive "less" than we otherwise might have, if we were walking closer to God!*

Here's the mistaken view. "Good and Bad," as stated above in this scripture, is a comparative phrase, <u>not one of opposite meaning</u>. It is better stated, "good and fallow," or, "good and not so good." The word "fallow" carries the meaning of, "marked by inactivity." <u>Again, a comparison of work</u>, <u>and no work</u>, or, <u>little work at best</u>. Also, to complete the correct understanding, "Bad" *(phaulon)* simply means... "worthless."

The single purpose of this Judgment is for God to reward His born-again believers for their service and their commitment in serving Him. Nothing more, nothing less! In the Christian world, there are those who have taken more seriously, the call of God on their life than others. God, in His judgment, will reward each one of us according to His view of our commitment in serving Him.

This wrongly held belief cannot be glossed over, but must be made clear to God's people who have been taught, in reality, to fear the Judgment Seat of Christ. It's not unlike the teachings of the Pharisees in forcing people to adhere to their rules and laws. This teaching is the opposite of Grace, God's Grace. It speaks of a requirement, or action the believer must adhere to, or face the music! In any event, God is the final judge on this kind of conduct, *(not this writer,)* by otherwise good people of God, who have simply somehow fallen prey to this false teaching.

The moment of truth at the Judgment Seat of Christ is not about sin, it's about service to God, or the work we do for Him. Heaven is to be a place of joy, not pain as some might errantly want us to believe. Good work will be rewarded, and bad or "worthless" work will be discarded.

Listen to what Scofield, the Bible commentator has to say on this matter.

"The judgment of the believer's works, not sins, is in question here. These have been atoned for, and are "remembered no more forever" Heb 10:17, but every work must come into judgment, Mt 12:36 Rom 14:10 Gal 6:7 Eph 6:8 Col 3:24, 25. The result is "reward" or "loss" (of the reward), "but he himself shall be saved" 1Cor 3:11-15." *Listen to the clear and undeniable words of this scripture.*

(For no one can lay any foundation other than the one already laid, which is Jesus Christ. If anyone builds on this foundation using gold, silver, costly stones, wood, hay or straw, their work will be shown for what it is, because the Day (Judgment Seat of Christ) will bring it to light. It will be revealed with fire, and the fire will test the quality of each person's work. If what has been built survives, the builder will receive a reward. If it is burned up, the builder will suffer loss but yet will be saved—even though only as one escaping through the flames.) (Added emphasis)

The rewards we receive will be placed at the feet of our Savior in love for Him. The "lost" rewards will never be made known. There is no room for Pharisaical Judgment by any one of us against another. *(Matthew chapter (7) is very clear on the whole subject of judging one another.)*

This is the central key to understanding this false teaching.

In conclusion of this subject, may I leave you with this thought an encouragement? God has chosen to provide rewards to those who love and serve Him. We cannot speculate on the final purpose of His decision to do this. We can then only believe it's His method to encourage action in sharing His love for all mankind.

He has commanded us to do this! It's not a request, but we are ordered to be ambassadors of His Grace and Love. This deserves thoughtful consideration, and should drive our commitment to be what we know we should be. But, again… it should be out of love, not fear.

"The Day of the Lord"

In approaching the final conclusion to this book, written and directed by the Spirit of God, as he has prompted these fingers to write, He has chosen the following scriptural references as a way of signaling you, the reader, of a day in the future which will put an end to this present world as we know it. That day, is known as…

"The Day of the Lord!"

Sitting here this morning, contemplating the day ahead with a cup of coffee in hand, I wondered about this all eventful day. For most, this will be a terrible and frightening day. A moment in time when "everything we know," means nothing. When our worst possible day of the past will now seem like Heaven on earth! This will be a day of distraction and death and a day of final endings. There will be no possible way out, no place of hiding or shelter, nor more time to reverse our attitudes, no more compassion, or unmerited love for us to consider or reject. No longer is the choice ours, it's over, no more time, the clock stops!

Since this date has not yet arrived, on what basis can you reject this truth of God's Word, and possibly feel confident that this is just another "fairytale" brought to life by old men who saw visions and made up these stories of future events?

Allow me to ask a second question. "Tell me, for what reason would all of the writers of the Word of God, over some 1600 years, who lived in the very presence of God, both Father and Son, have in compiling this sacred document of all documents. Tell me, if you will... what reason?" "What sensible person could attach a nefarious plan of some sort, for the development of this ultimate enlightenment of Past, Present and Future life on earth, called the Bible?"

Friend... The choice is still yours, at least for now. The "Day of the Lord" could happen at any future moment in time. Do not die in your sins, rather, choose to live in the light of His love.

Note: for the child of God, this day will not be experienced, or lived through! We will have already been raised to newness of life at the coming of Jesus in Glory. We will be either raised from the grave, or if still alive, we will meet Him in in His Glory...to forever be with Him in the New Heaven and the New Earth... this earth which will be changed and renewed to the sinless existence of God's original creation!

The Book of 2 Peter, chapter 3, is devoted to the above reality. It's a short, but a powerful and succinct revelation of coming judgment. Listen and absorb these impassioned words from one of the strongest followers of Jesus. He opens his letter showing his purpose in writing.

Dear friends, this is now my second letter to you. I have written both of them as reminders to stimulate you to wholesome thinking. I want you to recall the words spoken in the past by the holy prophets and the command given by our Lord and Savior through your apostles.

Above all, you must understand that in the <u>last days scoffers will come</u>, scoffing and following their own evil desires. They will say, "Where is this 'coming' he prom-

ised? Ever since our ancestors died, everything goes on as it has since the beginning of creation." But they deliberately forget that long ago by God's word the heavens came into being and the earth was formed out of water and by water. By these waters also the world of that time was deluged and destroyed. By the same word the present heavens and earth are reserved for fire, being kept for the Day of Judgment and destruction of the ungodly.

Peter knew their thinking, even in that day, and up until now, we can see the truth of these words. *He continues...*

But do not forget this one thing, dear friends: With the Lord a day is like a thousand years, and a thousand years are like a day. The Lord is not slow in keeping his promise, as some understand slowness. Instead he is patient with you, <u>not wanting anyone to perish</u>, <u>but everyone to come to repentance</u>.

But the day of the Lord will come like a thief. The heavens will disappear with a roar; the elements will be destroyed by fire, and the earth and everything done in it will be laid bare.

Since everything will be destroyed in this way, what kind of people ought you to be? You ought to live holy and godly lives as you look forward to the day of God and speed its coming. That day will bring about the destruction of the heavens by fire, and the elements will melt in the heat. But in keeping with his promise we are looking forward to a new heaven and a new earth, where righteousness dwells.

The following then is this...the "Mea Culpa," or a short summation of our responsibility.

So then, dear friends, since you are looking forward to this, make every effort to be found spotless, blameless and at peace with him. Bear in mind that our Lord's patience means salvation, just as our dear brother Paul also wrote you with the wisdom that God gave him. He writes the same way in all his letters, speaking in them of these matters. His letters contain some things that are hard to understand, which ignorant and unstable people distort, as they do the other Scriptures, to their own destruction.

Therefore, dear friends, <u>since you have been forewarned</u>, be on your guard so that you may not be carried away by the error of the lawless and fall from your secure position. But grow in the grace and knowledge of our Lord and Savior Jesus Christ. To him be glory both now and forever! Amen. (2 Peter 3: 1-18)

As Peter continues to speak to his fellow believers, he reminds them of the patience of God, a patience which is not unlike a "door stop." The door to salvation and eternity with God is still open, but the day is coming... "The Day of the Lord," when the doorstop is removed, and it's all over, those of you who have walked through the door need to be on your guard and not allow false teachers to try and draw you away from the truth, only found in the Word of God.

"Our Faithful God"

In culmination of the writing of these two books, MSM, and MMSM, on the "Power and Purpose of Faith," on the last day prior to the sending of this manuscript to the publisher, I witnessed once again the leading hand of God, in a very specific way in telling me precisely what he wanted me to write in concluding this book.

Like every other day, I grabbed a cup of coffee and sat down with my faithful and beautiful wife Gale, to enjoy her presence as well as the presence of God as we studied and prayed together about those things which were on our minds for this day. As I picked up my study Bible, and opened it to the 17th chapter of Matthew, *(my typical routine each morning, is to read one chapter, along with all of the supporting commentary for every verse in that chapter.)* a chapter which tells the story of Peter, James and John and the call to them by Jesus to participate in His "Transfiguration," and to learn from Jesus, that John the Baptist was the predicted embodiment of Elijah, *(Malachi 4:5)* then, to have once again, the opportunity to be taught a lesson by the "Master," Jesus my Redeemer, regarding the very essence of faith.

When you read this chapter in Matthew, you'll discover several stories regarding Jesus' power to heal. One in particular caught my eye, and was about the man who was concerned about his "Demon possessed son" which the disciples were unable to remove from him. When they asked Jesus why they were powerless to do this, after having been given the power of healing, from Jesus...

He replied, "Because you have so little faith. I tell you the truth, if you have faith as small as a <u>mustard seed</u>, you can say to this mountain, "move from here to there" and it will move. Nothing will be impossible for you. (Matthew 17:20)
(Added emphasis)

Jesus wasn't condemning His Disciples for weak faith, he was using this example to cement in their minds, and ours, the "meaning and power of faith." When faced with impossible situations, we should take our eyes off "The Mountain" and through faith, look to Jesus, not out of fear, or as the last resort, but out of "Believing Faith" in the power of God to perform miracles.

Faith is not faith, when we "predict the outcome, in advance of our prayer to God," or when we pray a weak or false prayer, out of duty.

God expects His children to expect miracles... Not performed and wrought by the power of their ability to pray, but by their humble faith in God, knowing he alone has the ability to answer.

Every prayerful request we make by faith, God listens to. In every instance, the outcome is of His choosing, because he alone knows the beginning from the end.

May the life experiences you've read in MSM, and how God was in charge of it all... and then to see the proclamation of God's Word in this book, MMSM, in bringing Biblical confirmation and truth to your heart and soul... be an encouragement as you measure your life against that which God wants for you.

Thank you dear friend, and... May the Peace of God reign in your heart and soul!

EPILOGUE

We Begin to Finish

"This is where YOU hit the road!"

It's graduation time! Whether you're 6 or 60 years old, it's your time to sprout wings, not as you might imagine the Angels have, but it's time to be on the move for God. To catch a glimpse daily, of what you need to do to satisfy His promptings in your life. These are promptings, which sometimes will scare the tar out of you, but also, with the knowledge that whatever fear you may have is removed when you take action. Will you make mistakes? Of course, but where there are no mistakes, there is no action!

You'll note the headline above, is very similar to the headline of the Epilogue in MSM. The words are just reversed. Remember… "We Finish to Begin" The idea in MSM was to begin a new life in Christ, and to build your own family of believers to carry the torch into the future. Here, "We Begin to Finish!" The idea is to develop an active working faith, built on an ever-increasing knowledge of God's Word. To see others make the same step of faith which you accomplished, and to see them grow as you see yourself grow in practical life terms and spiritual accomplishments, too numerous to consider!

As I come to the conclusion of this most joyful experience I've had in years, I seek your help in sharing this book with others, and encouraging them to do the same. *One last parting thought.*

"Because of you... Lord Jesus!"

A Prayer of Appreciation!

One day soon, I know I will stand in your presence. I know I will be able to speak to you in a Heavenly language. I will be able look you in the eye, face-to-face, and finally realize what a *Blessed Mountaintop Experience* is. I know I will experience love like never before. Then the excitement of understanding... finally, what "eternity" means. What the "New Heaven," and "New Earth" is. To understand the "New Purpose," you have in store for me. Then to, once and for all time, Heavenly time, have no knowledge of sin, a word missing from this new language. To be part of your eternal family, a family provided with Godly Purpose, Power and Glory because of your promises...

As children of God, and the "New Kingdom..." we shall be like you, equal, yet not equal; to be love filled because there will not be any room for "unloving;" to be in constant incomprehensible Godly light, and to travel the expanse of your never ending Universe, accomplishing your specific Will and Purpose; to be joined by, and rub shoulders with all Born Again Believers... from the first one you've chosen, to the last, including all of my earthly family, personal and extended members, which I've been privileged to share in the love of Jesus Christ on this Earthly stopover from birth, to my own personal re-birth in God.

"What all of this will be is not now for me to see!"
But I'm assured, through your "Word," it's true...
"Because of You... Lord Jesus!"

By the Author...Robert Hugh Park

Invitation:

I f you found this book to be of value in some personal way, I would love to hear from you! I fully realize this invitation flies in the face of all the standard protocol in writing, but "yours truly" has always been a maverick in this regard.

To contact me, my e-mail address is rpark1@neo.rr.com

If you have any disagreement with what is taught here, it's not my desire to discuss those differences, but, if God has spoken to you, I would like to meet you later... on the phone, if that fits your desire! Remember we will be rubbing shoulders in Heaven sooner than we all may think! I look forward to your e-mail.

May God Bless,
Robert Hugh *(Bob)* Park

Notes

There are a total of 161 Biblical references, including numerous individual scriptures...

(9) KJV
(1) NKJV
(2) NASB

The remaining 149 are taken from the NIV, 1984 edition.

Acknowledgements

Without the dedicated understanding and editing help from my wonderful wife Gale, I wouldn't have been able to make the publishing deadline!
Thank you, Sweetheart!

[1]Share Jesus without Fear, Author, William Fay with Linda Evans
Published by B&H Publishing Group, Nashville, TN
978-0-8054-1839-2

[2]Canton Baptist Temple, Canton Ohio
Christian Hall of Fame, used by permission.

[3]Wally Stuchul, used by permission.

CPSIA information can be obtained at www.ICGtesting.com
Printed in the USA
LVOW061128100212

268091LV00002B/9/P